The Splendor of Centennial Park

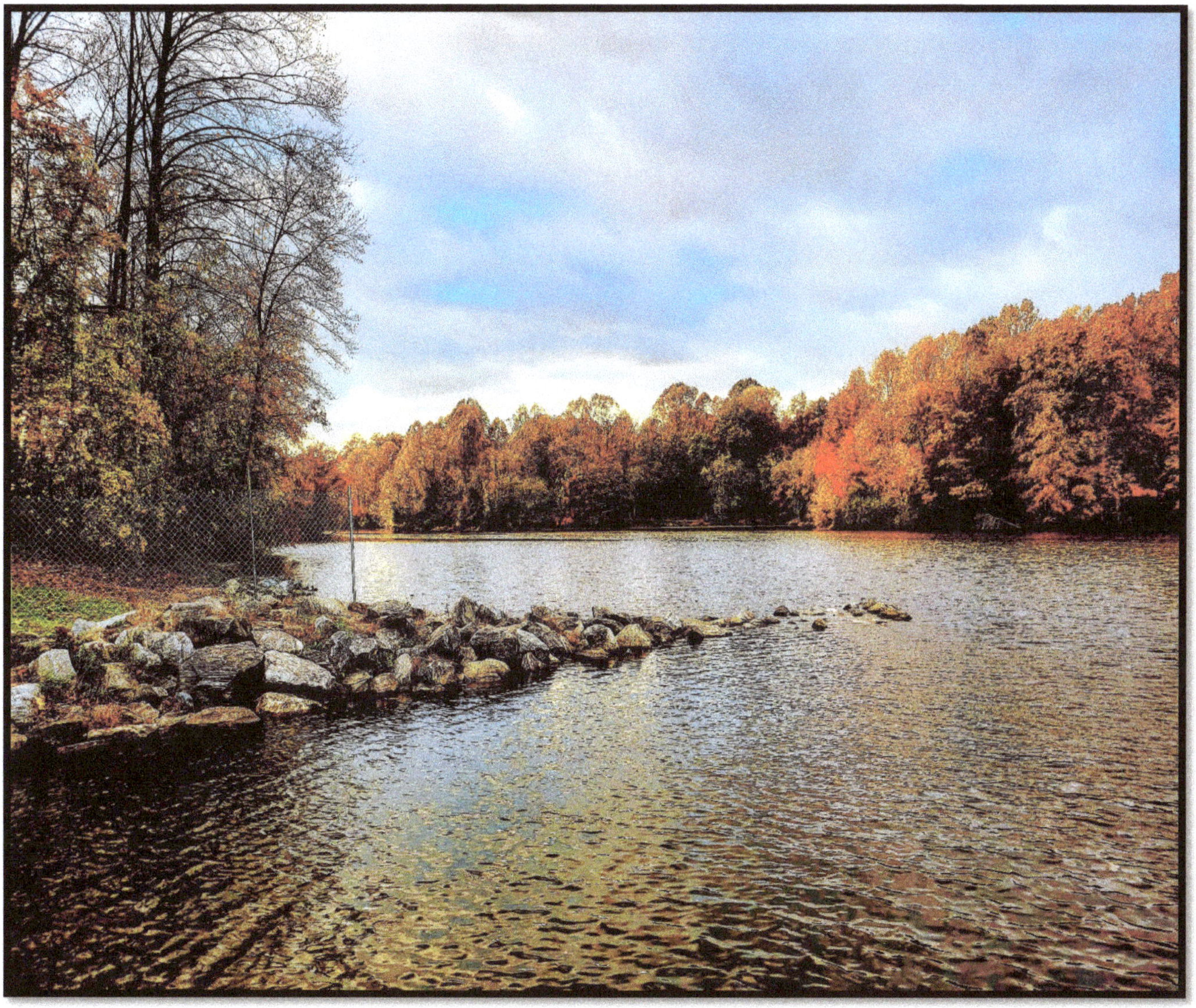

Wynette McKenzie

Publisher's Note: The photographs in this book were taken
at Centennial Park in Ellicott City, MD.
All photographs were taken by Wynette McKenzie.

The Splendor of Centennial Park© by Wynette McKenzie 2022

Photographs© by Wynette McKenzie

ISBN 978-1-941726-51-8

Five Little Angels Publishing.

All photographs by Wynette McKenzie.

Copyright 2022 by Five Little Angels, LLC.

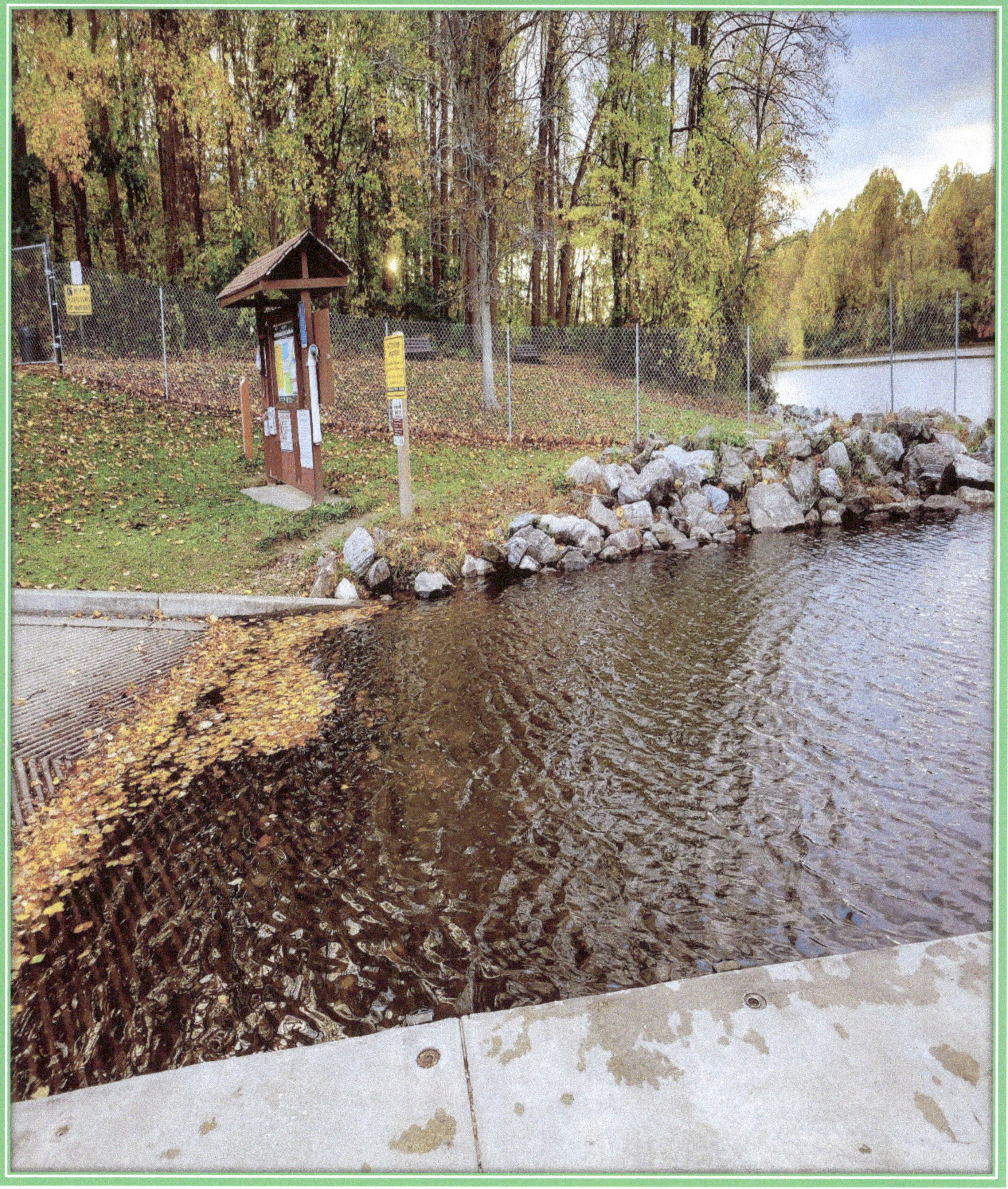

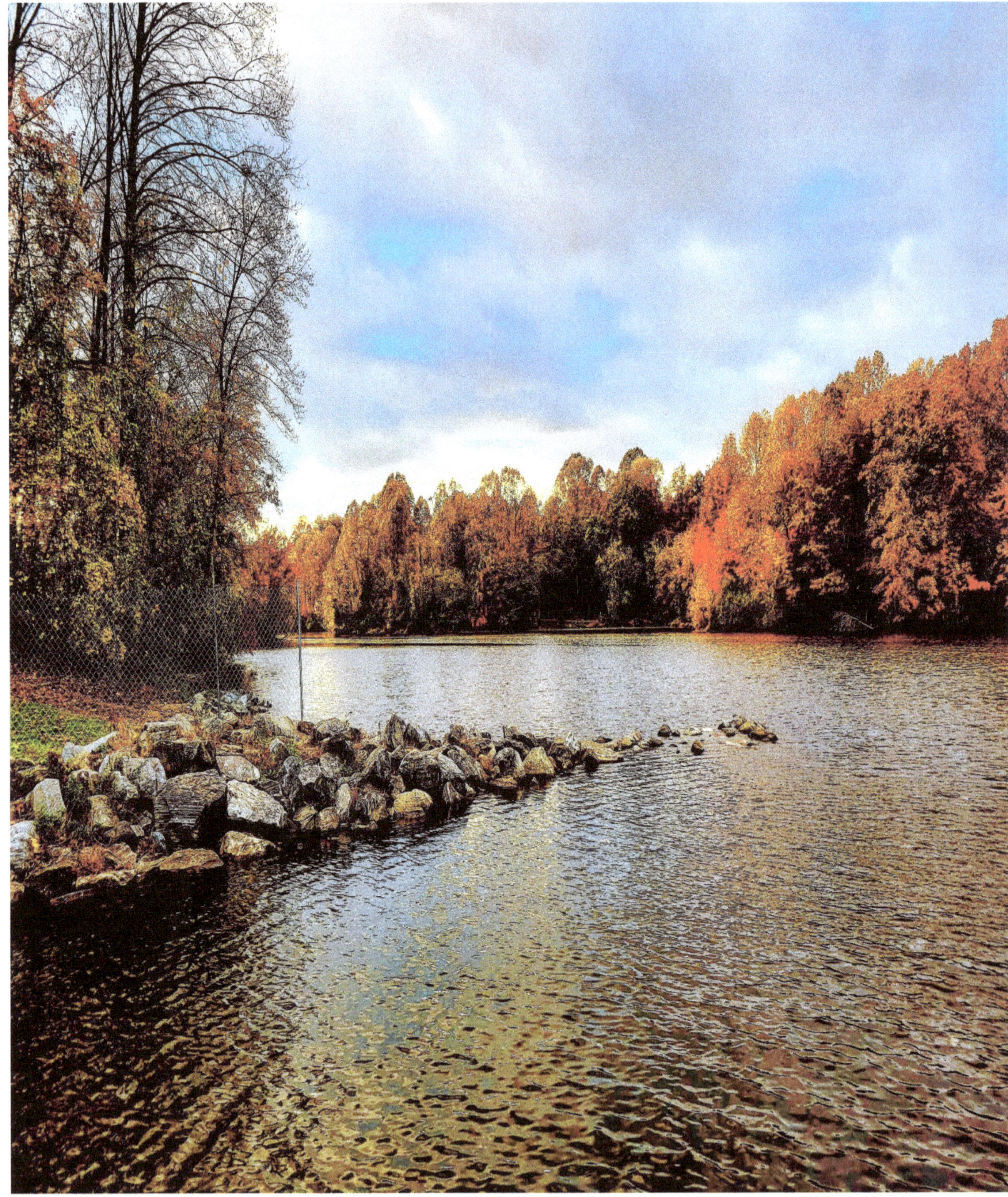

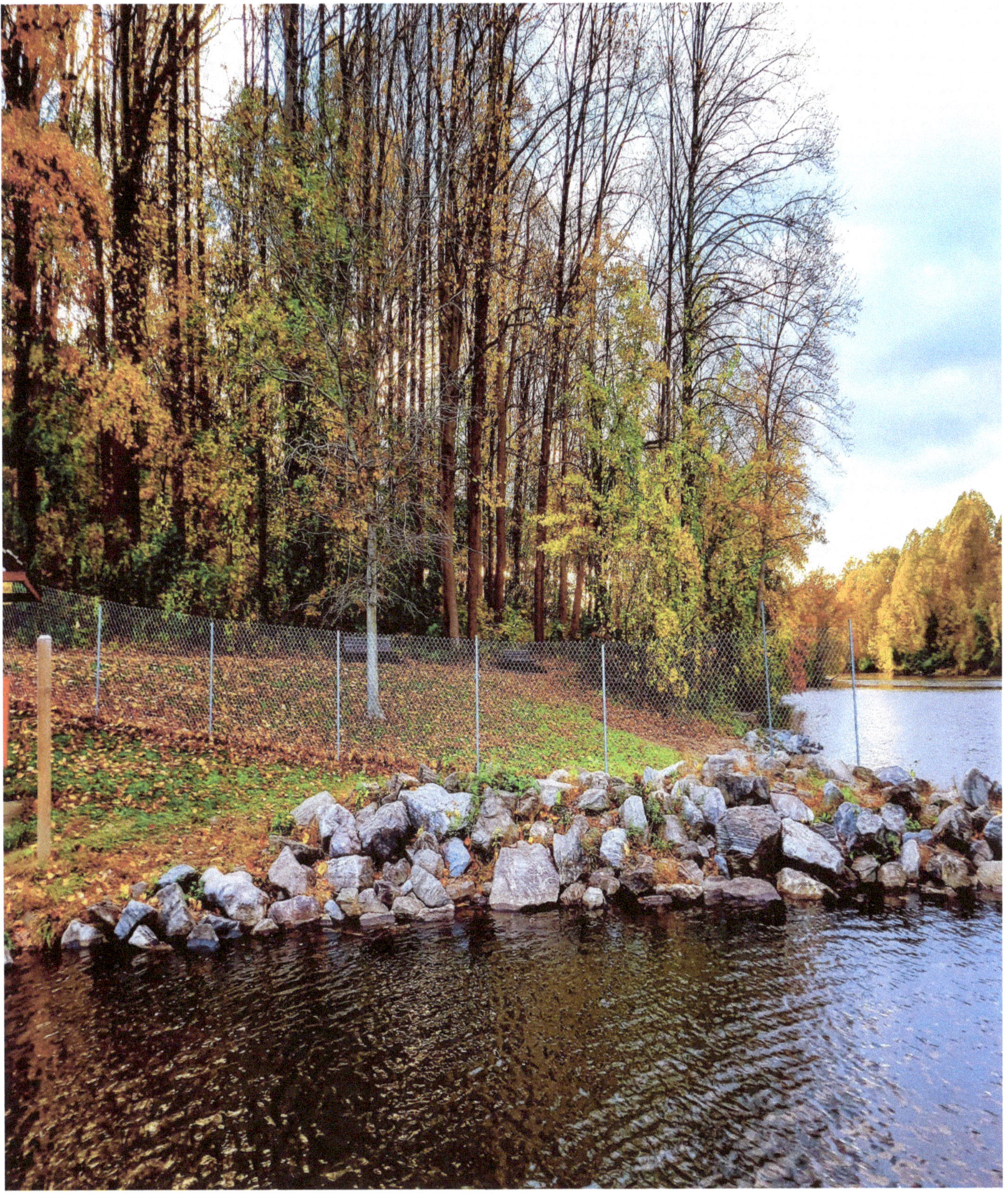

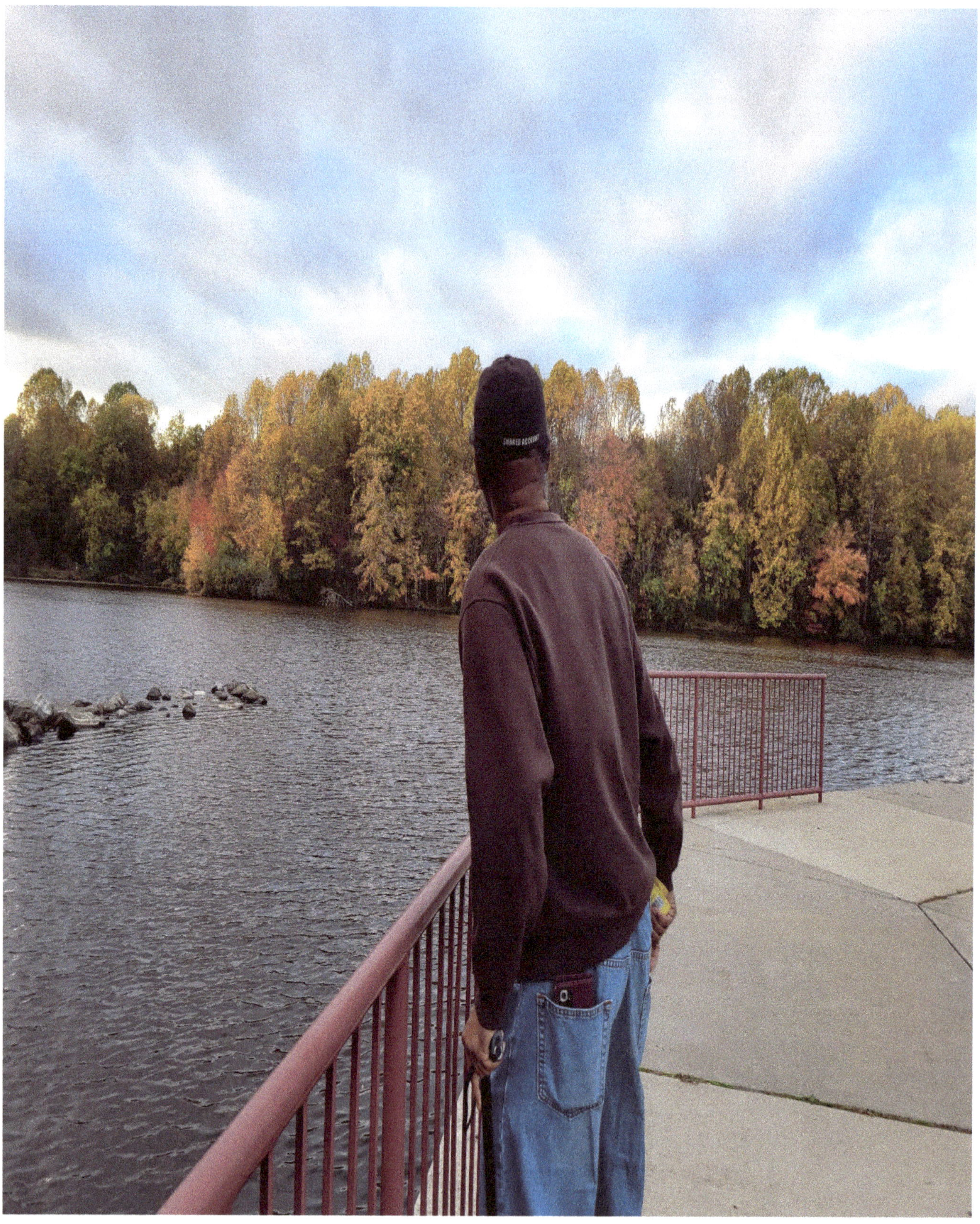

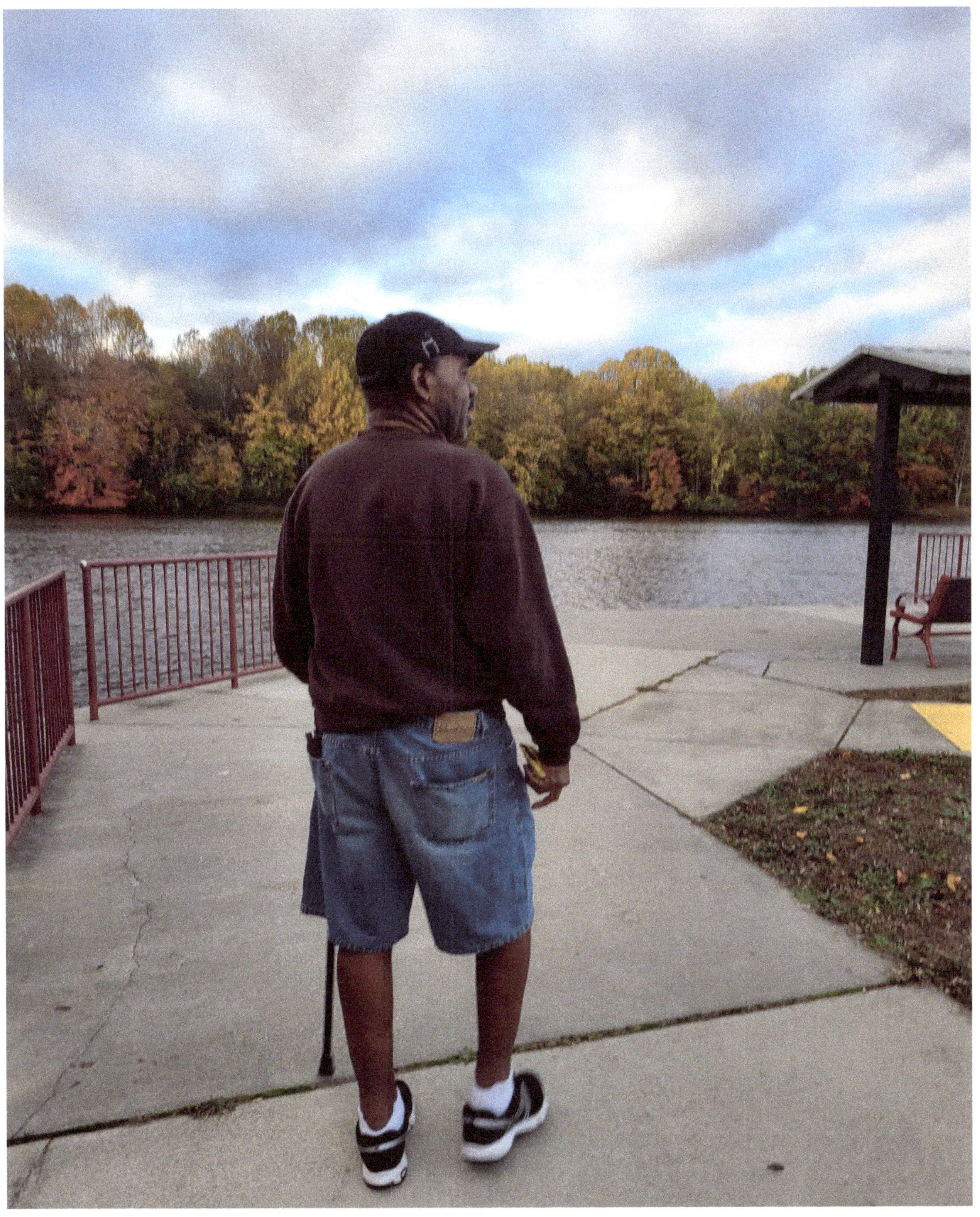

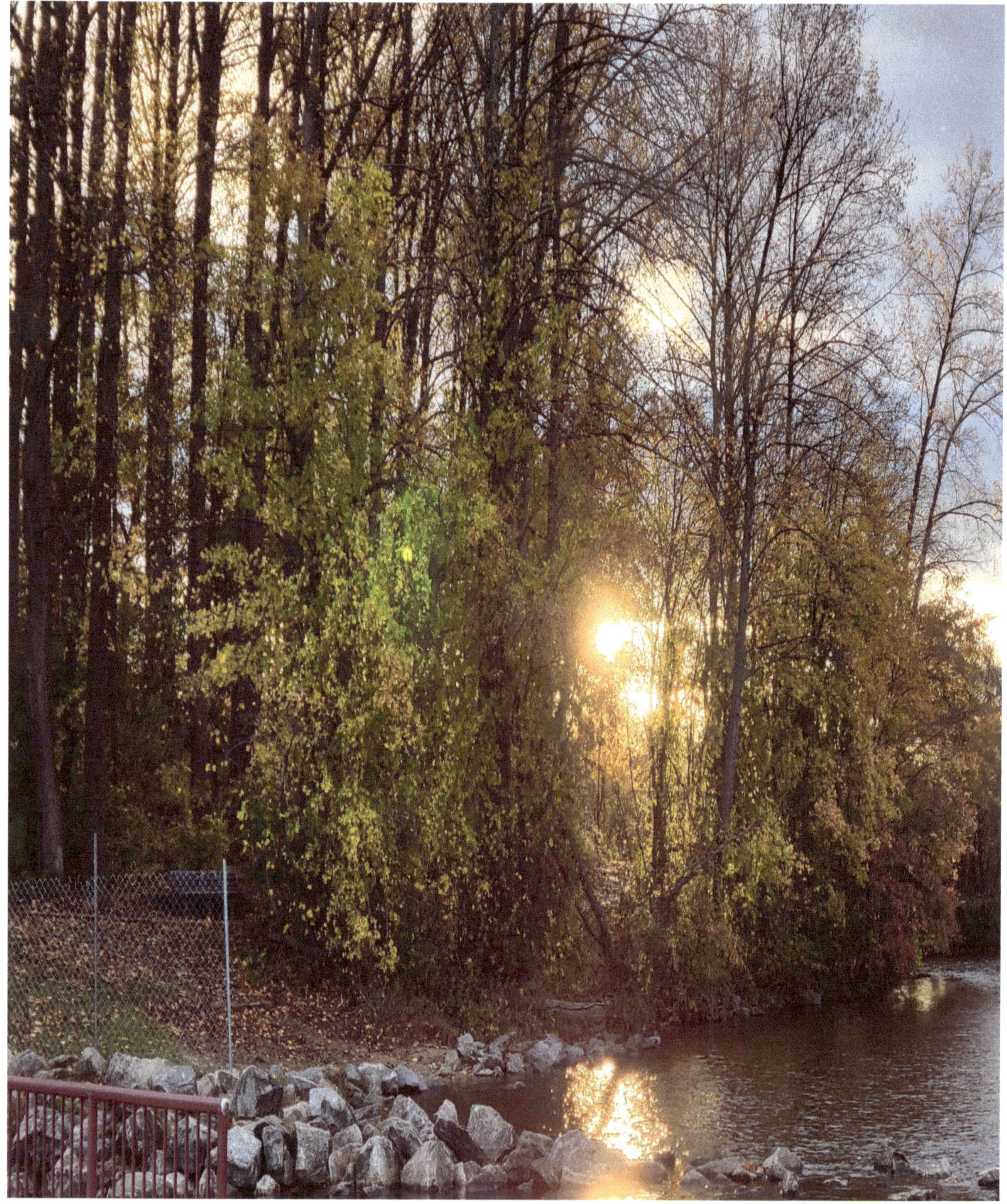

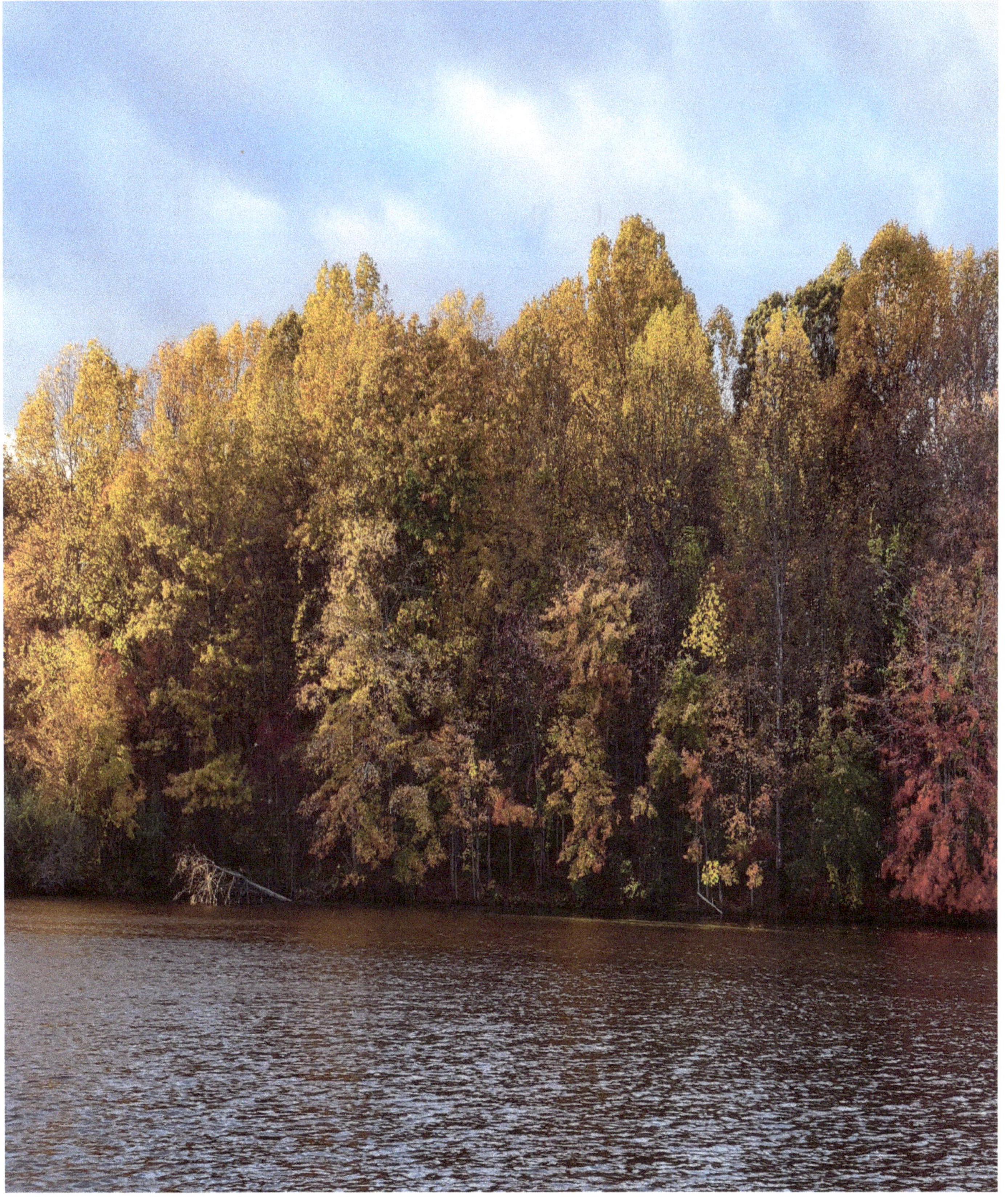

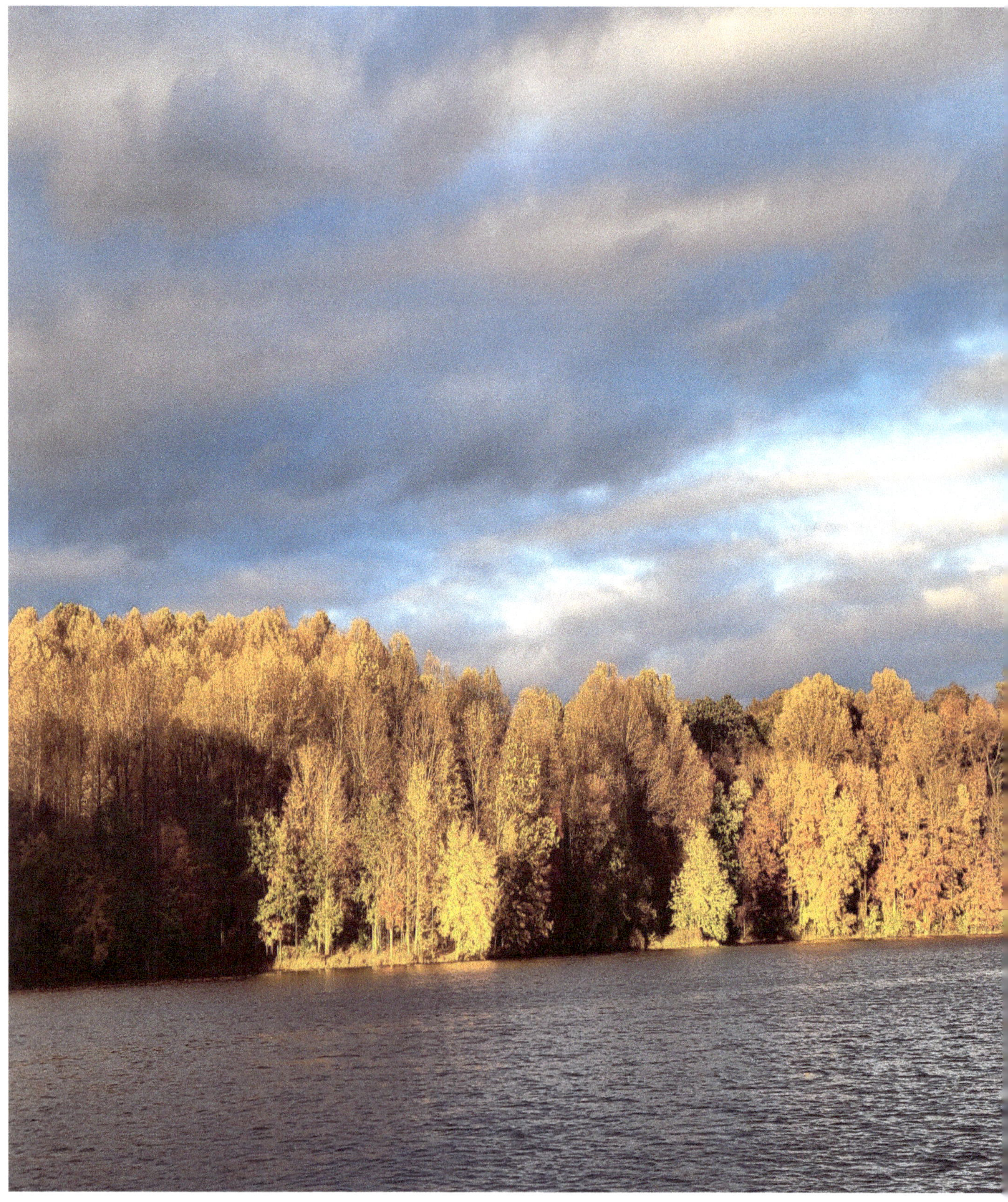

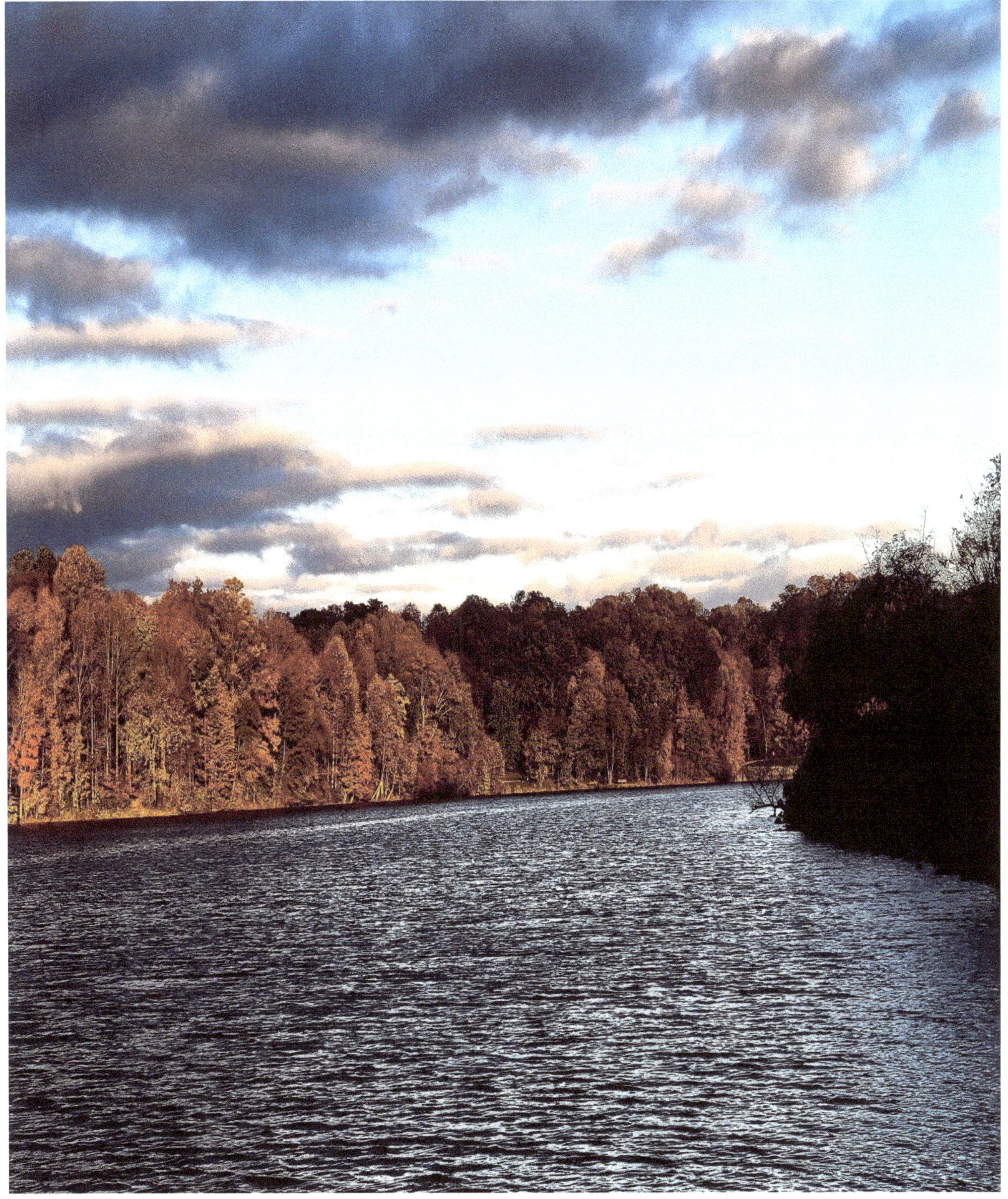

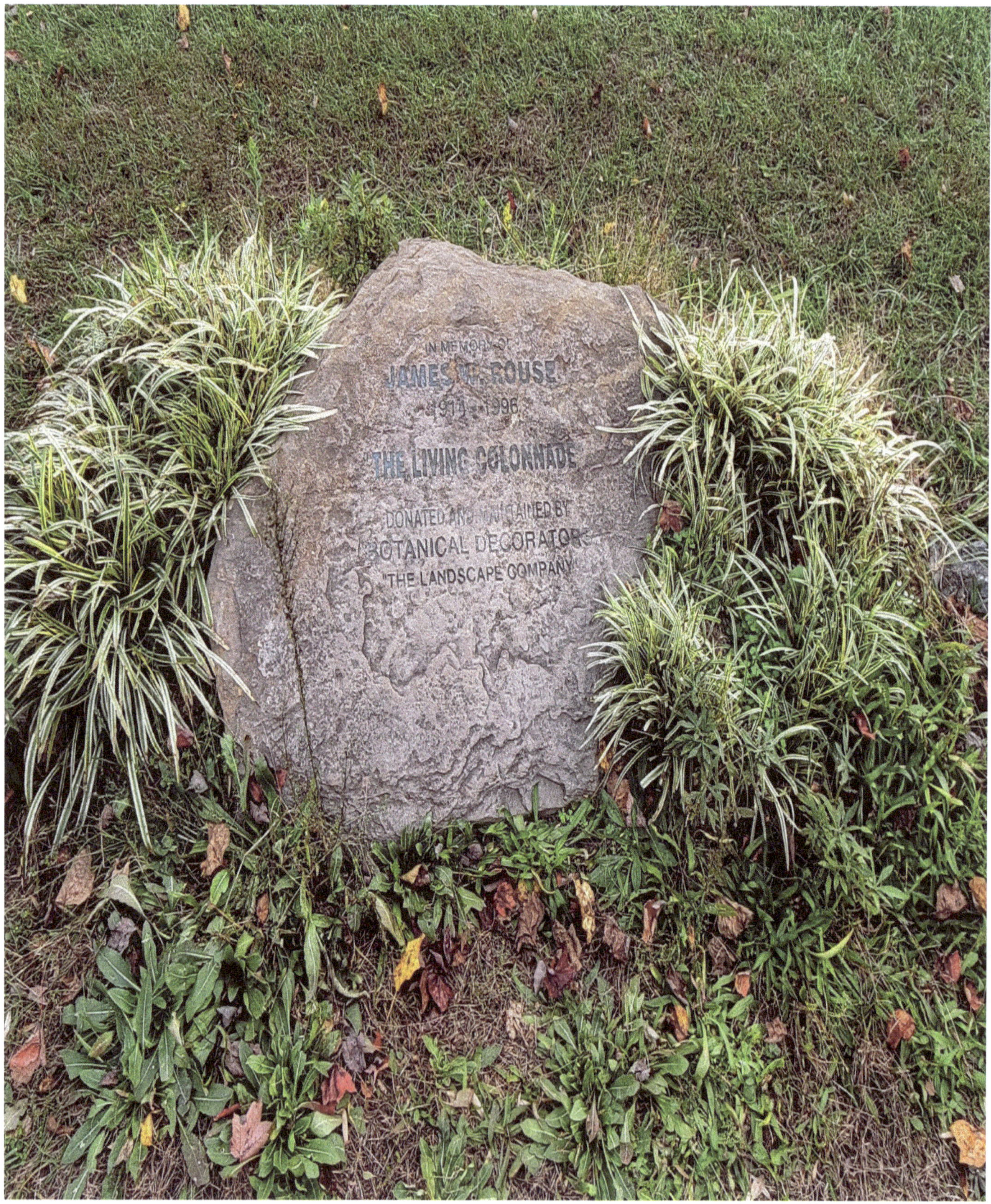

IN MEMORY OF
JAMES W. ROUSE
1914 - 1996
"THE LIVING COLONNADE"
DONATED AND MAINTAINED BY
BOTANICAL DECORATORS
"THE LANDSCAPE COMPANY"

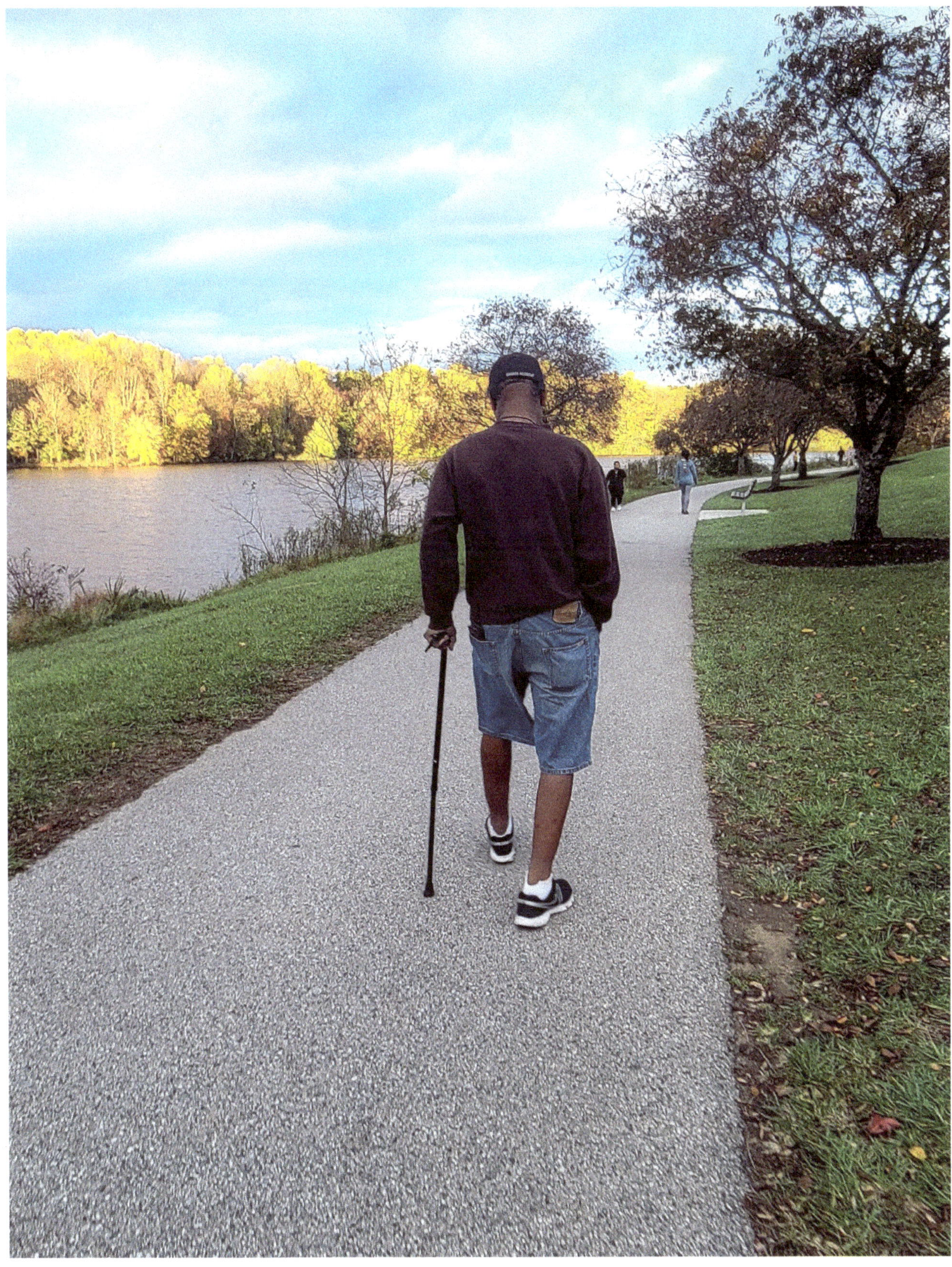

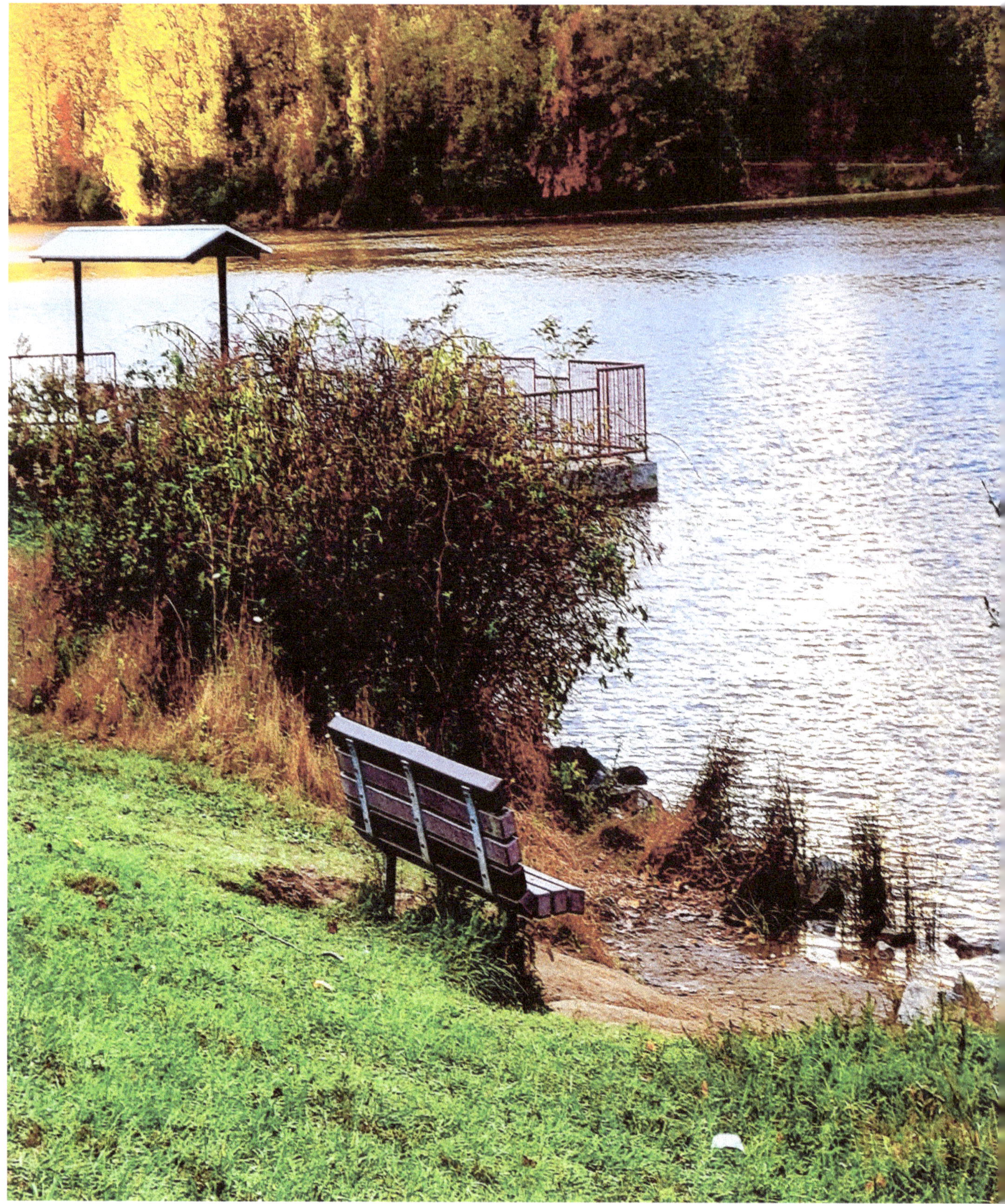

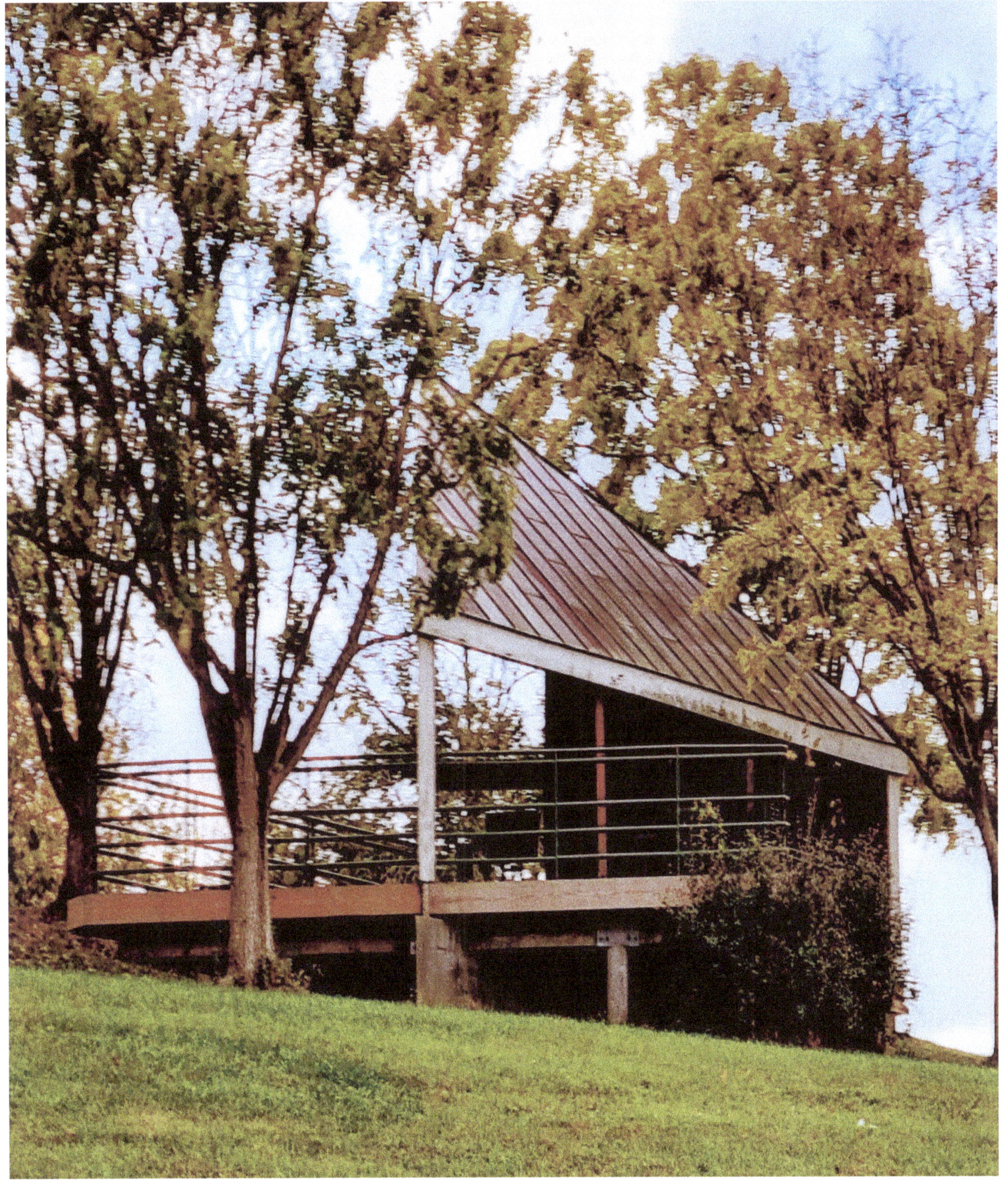

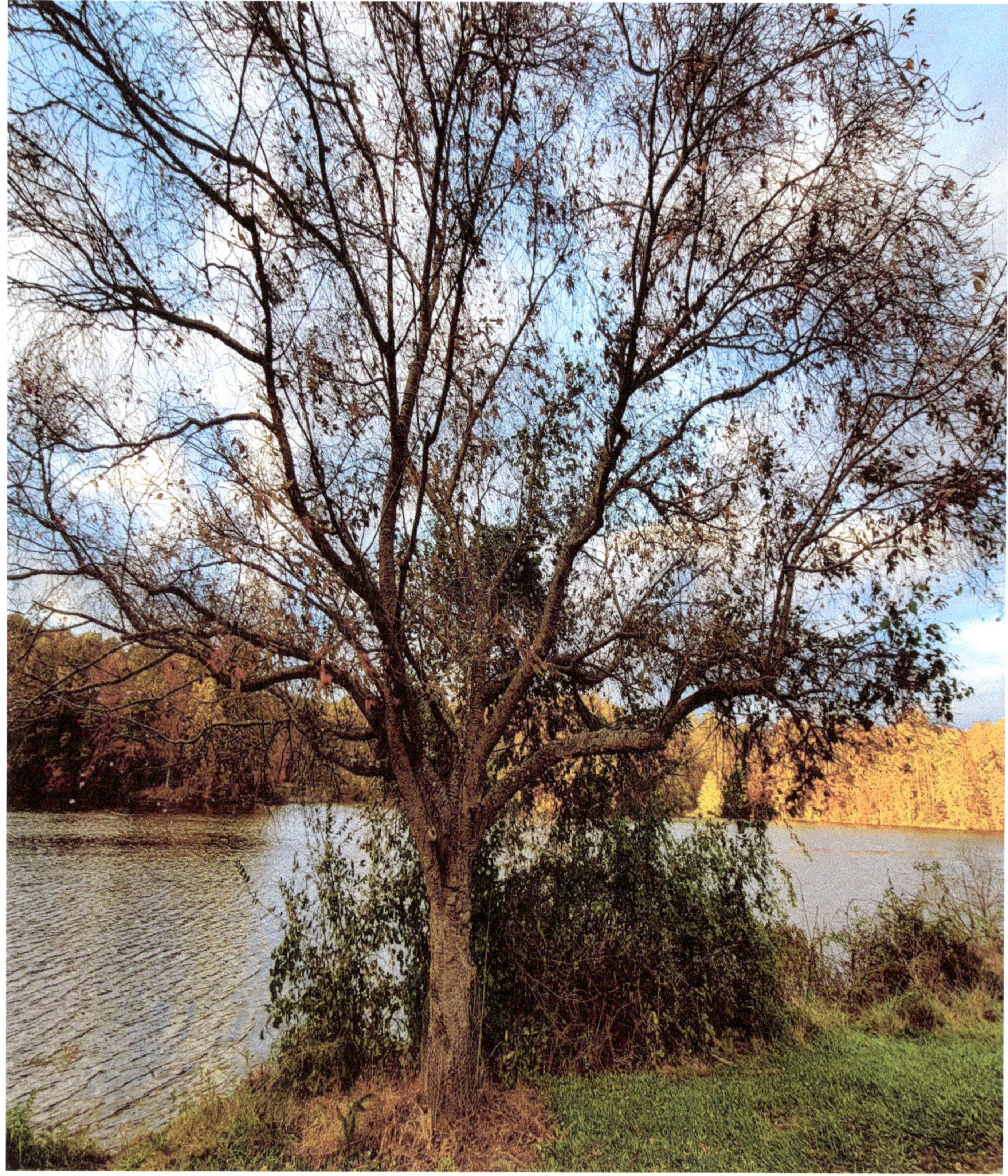

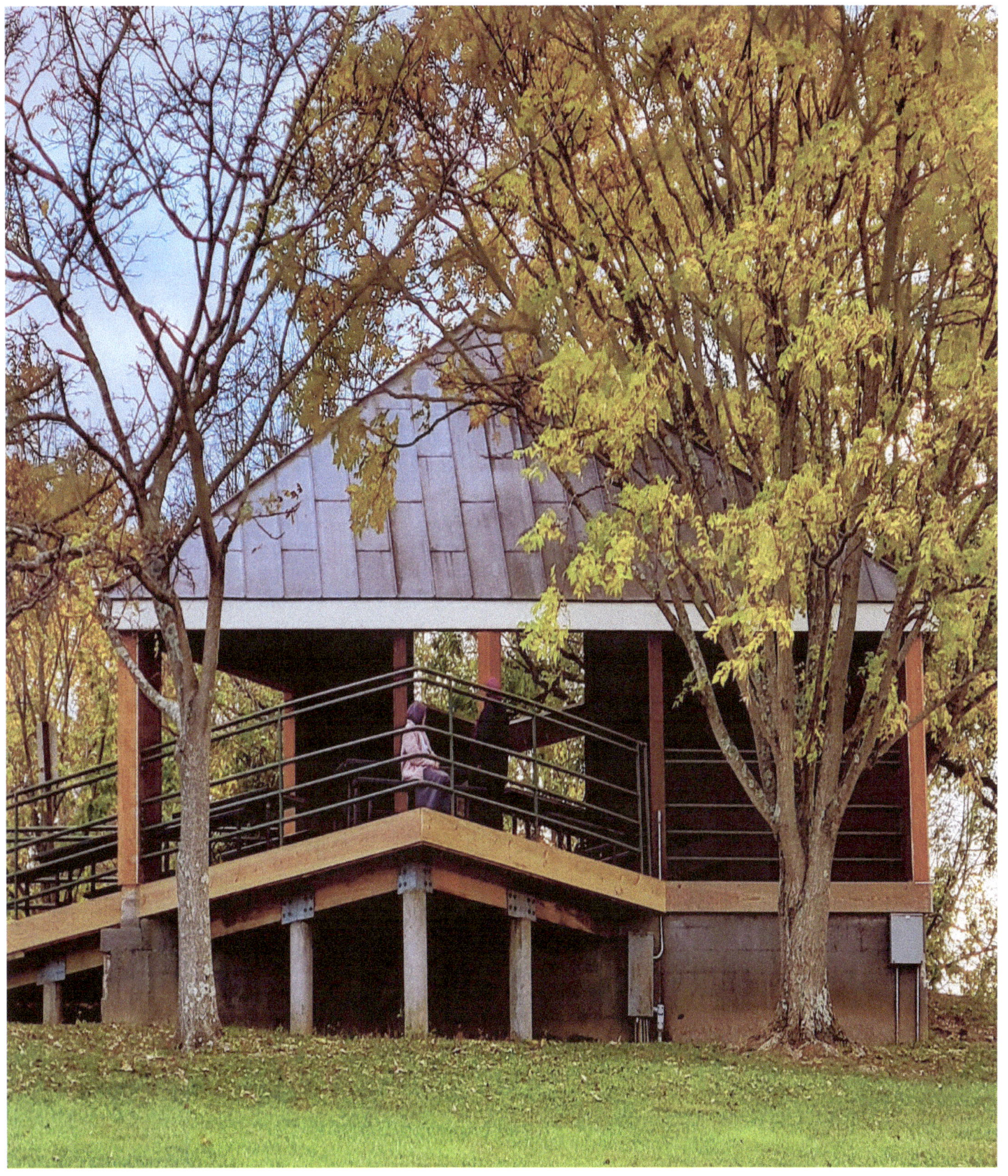

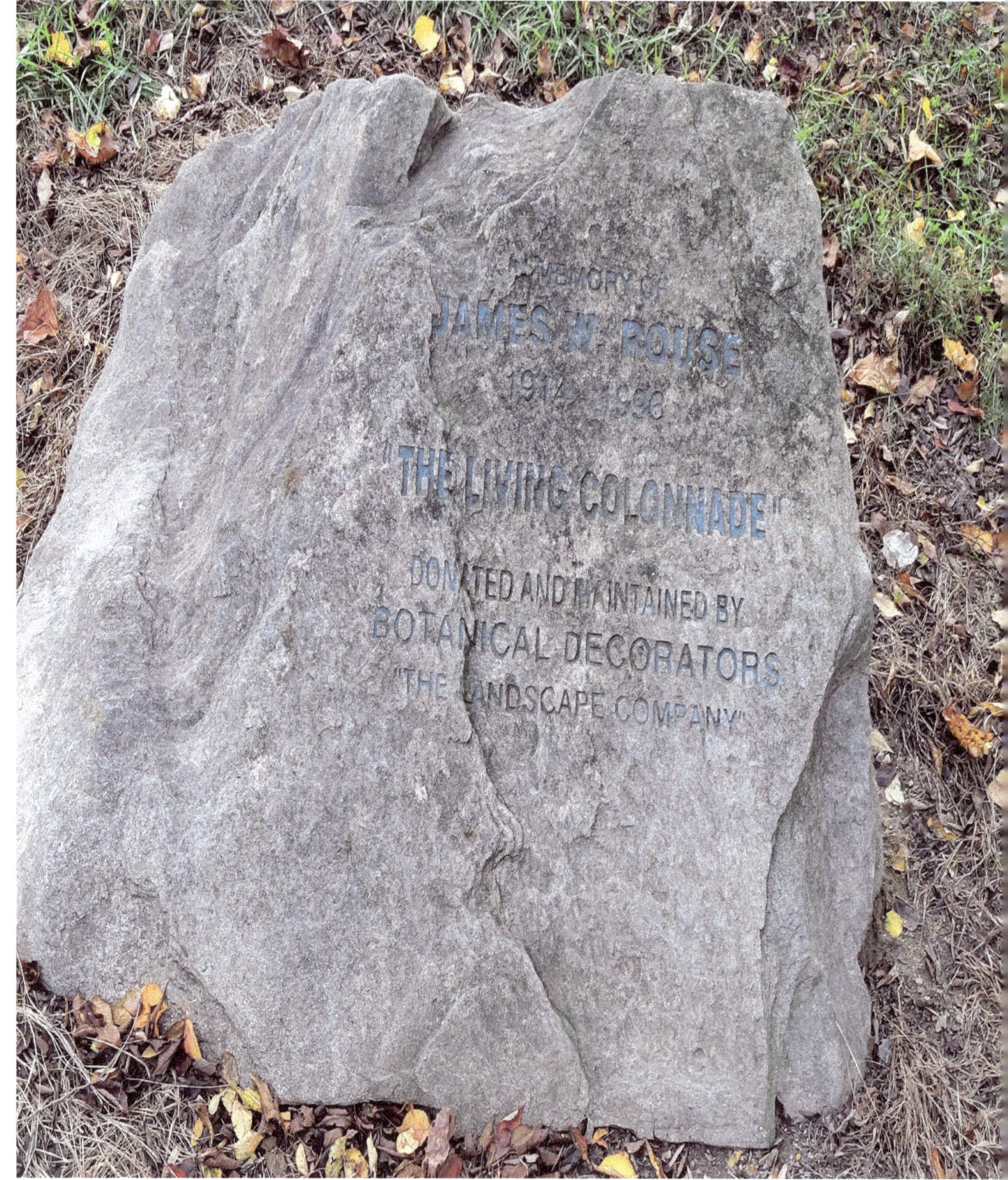

IN MEMORY OF
JAMES W. ROUSE
1914 - 1996
"THE LIVING COLONNADE"
DONATED AND MAINTAINED BY
BOTANICAL DECORATORS
"THE LANDSCAPE COMPANY"

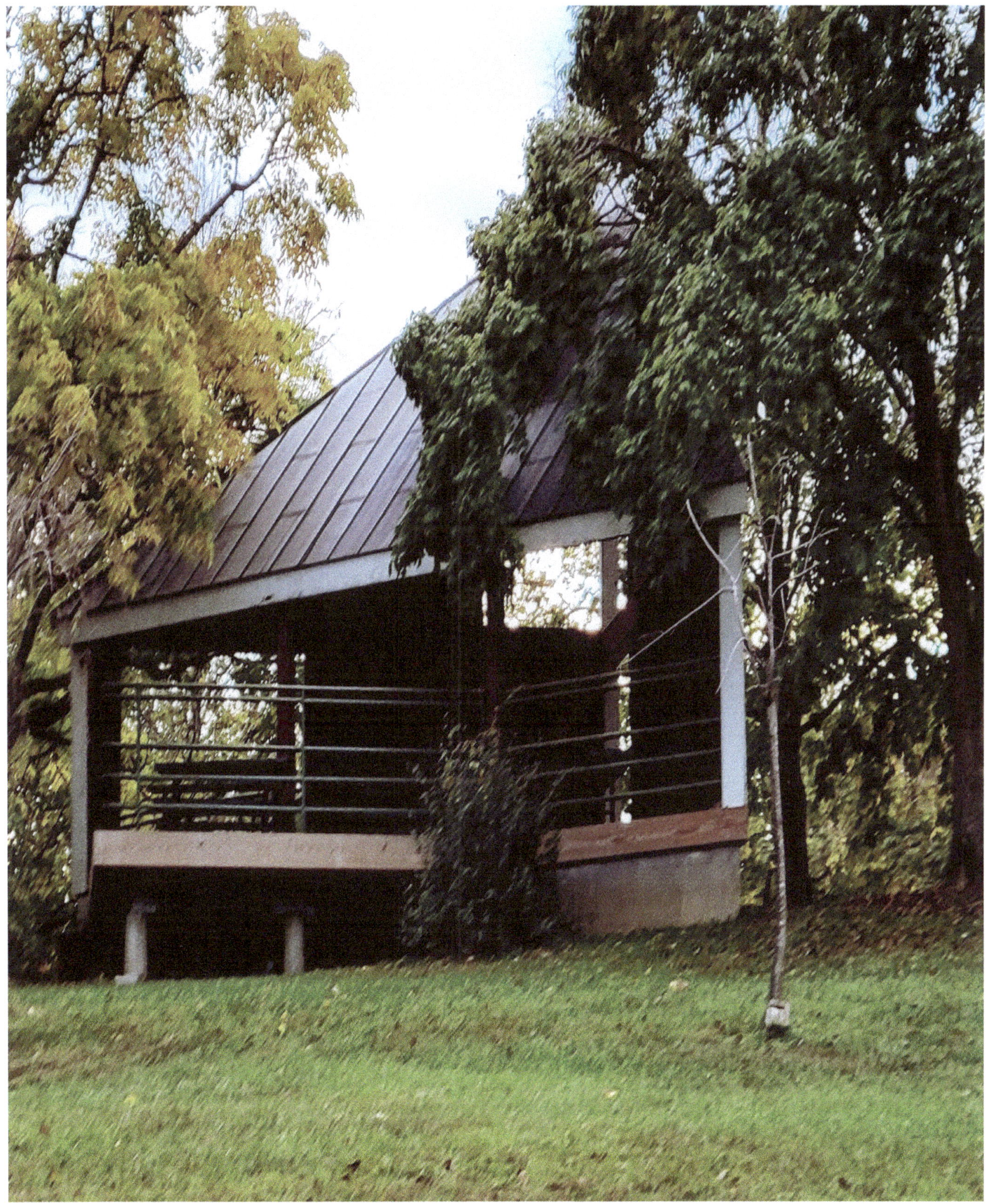

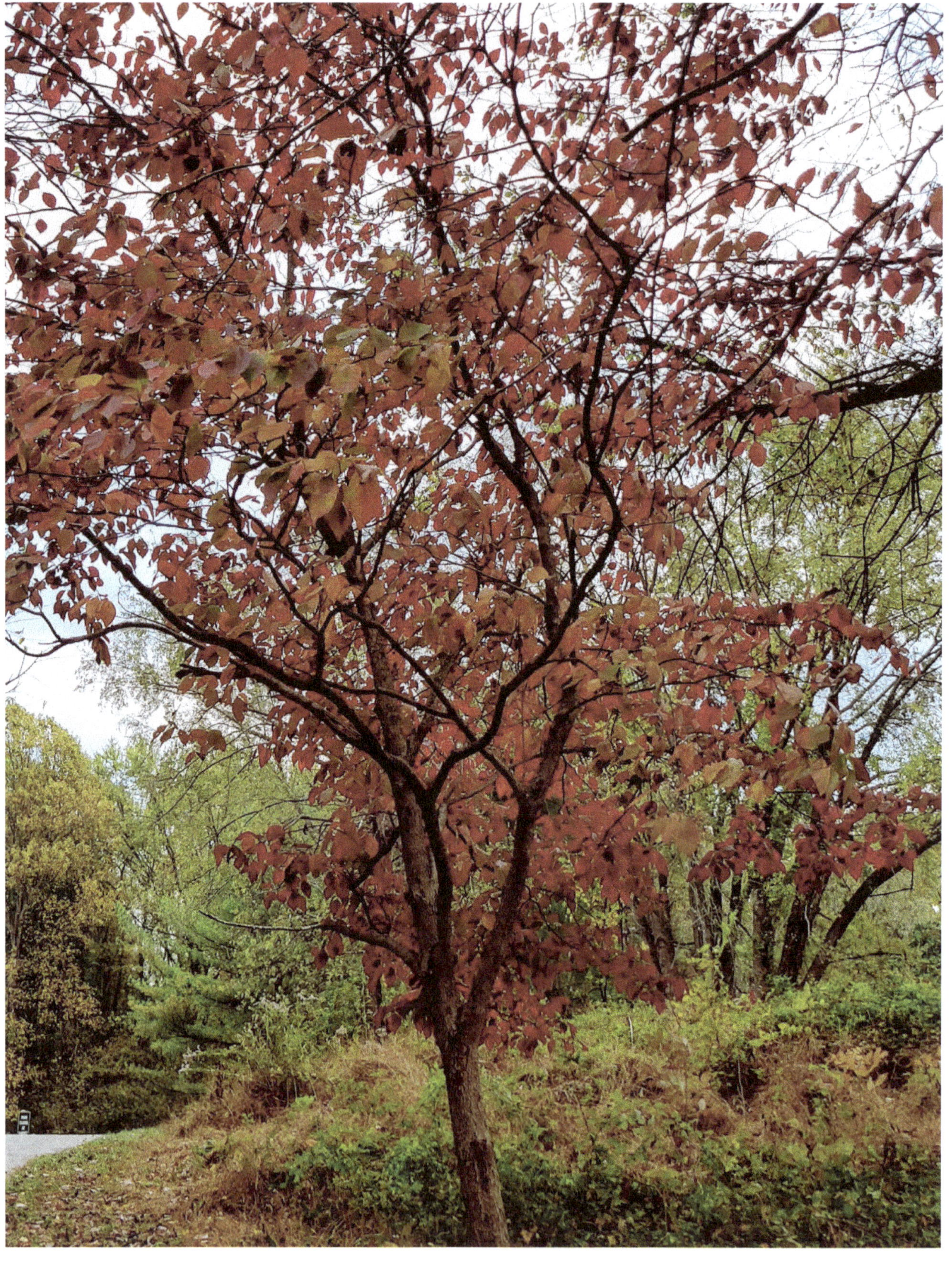

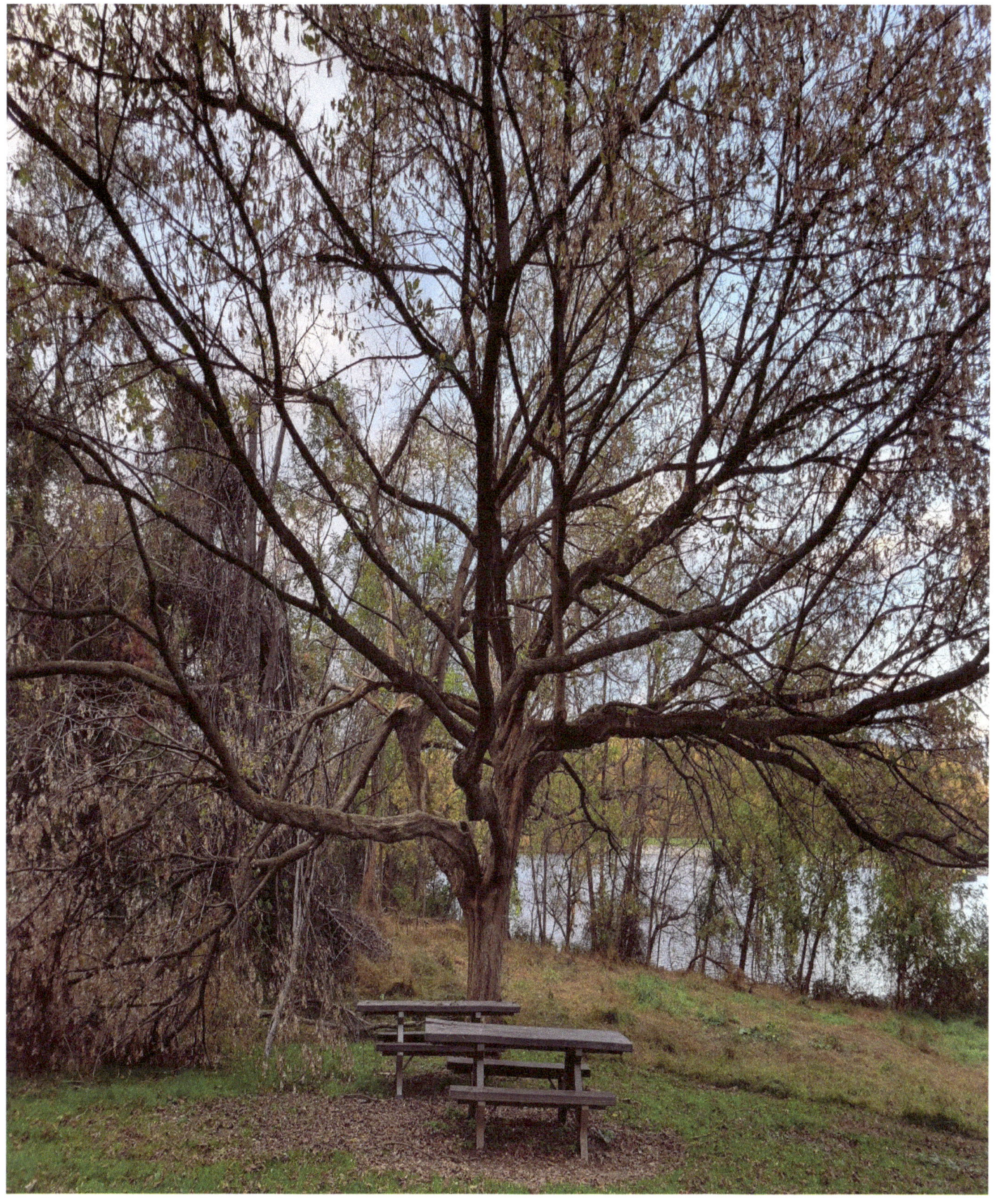

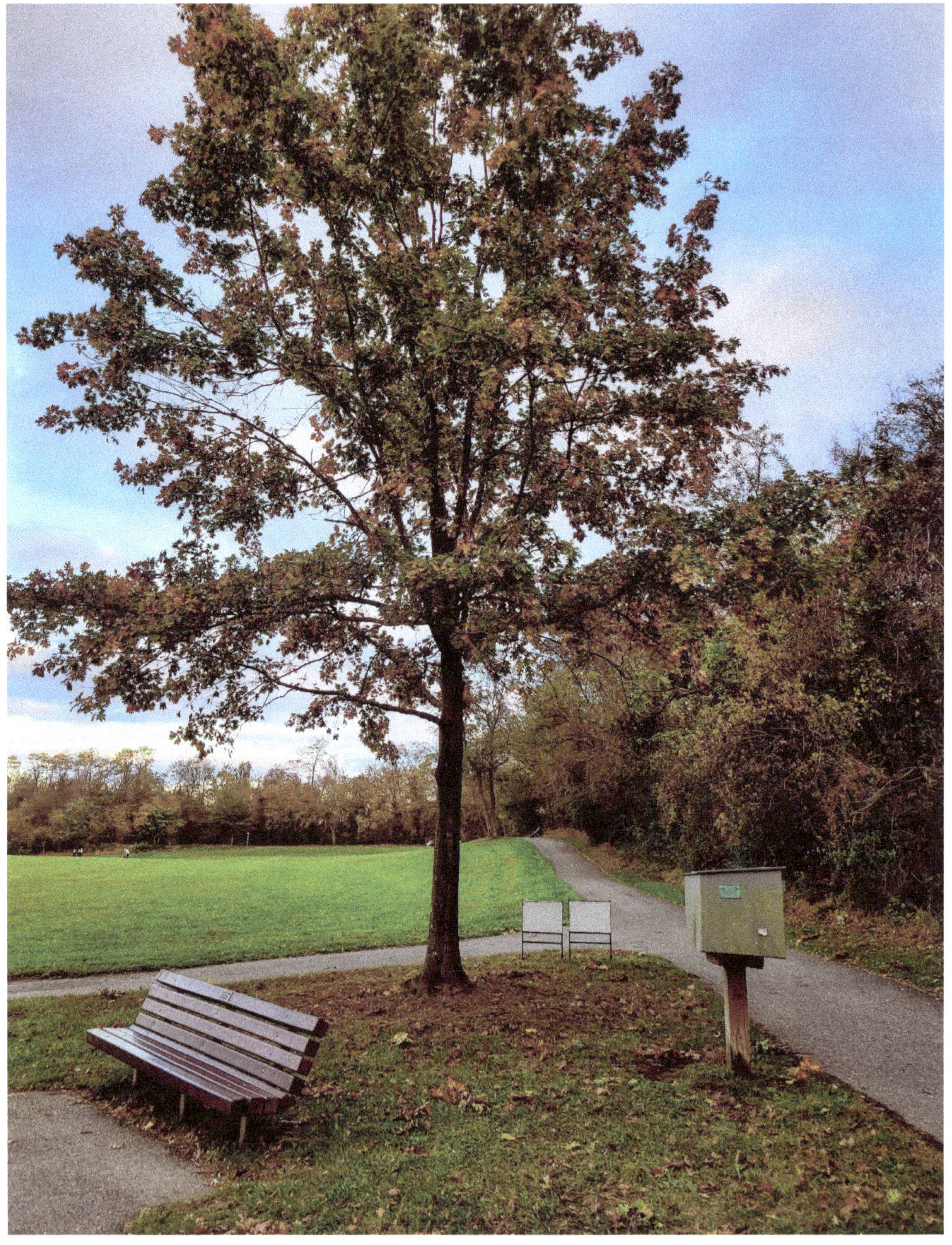

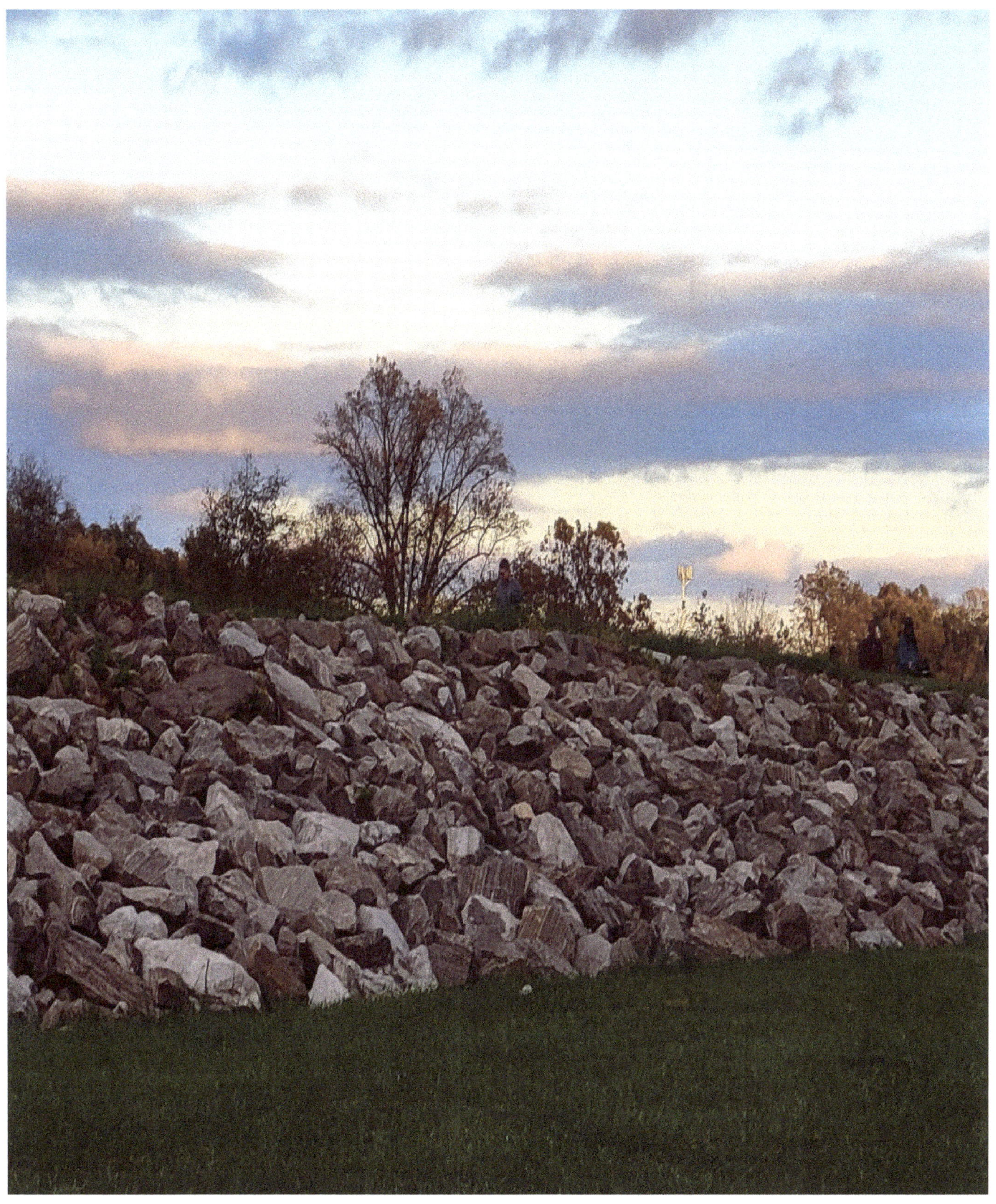

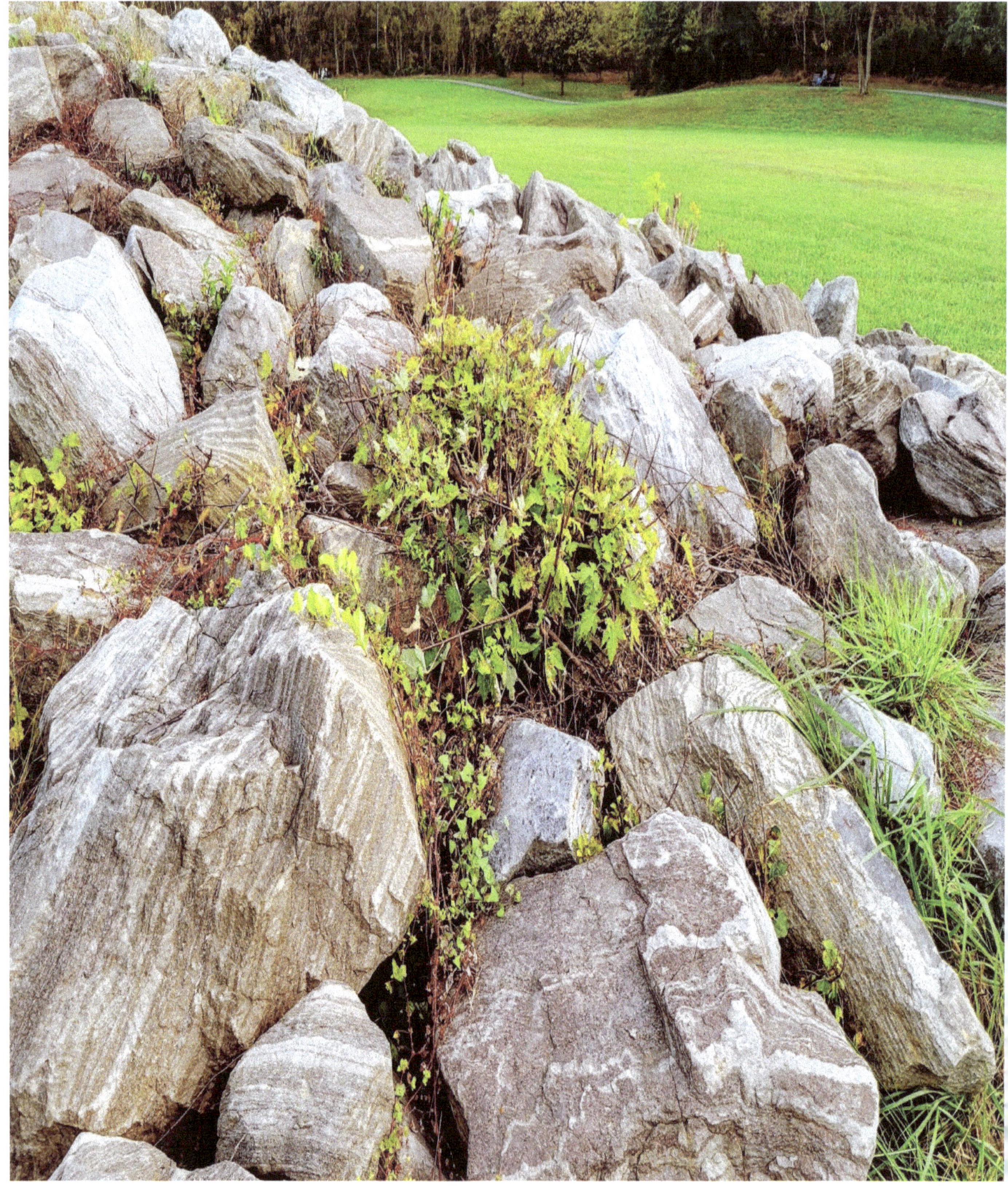

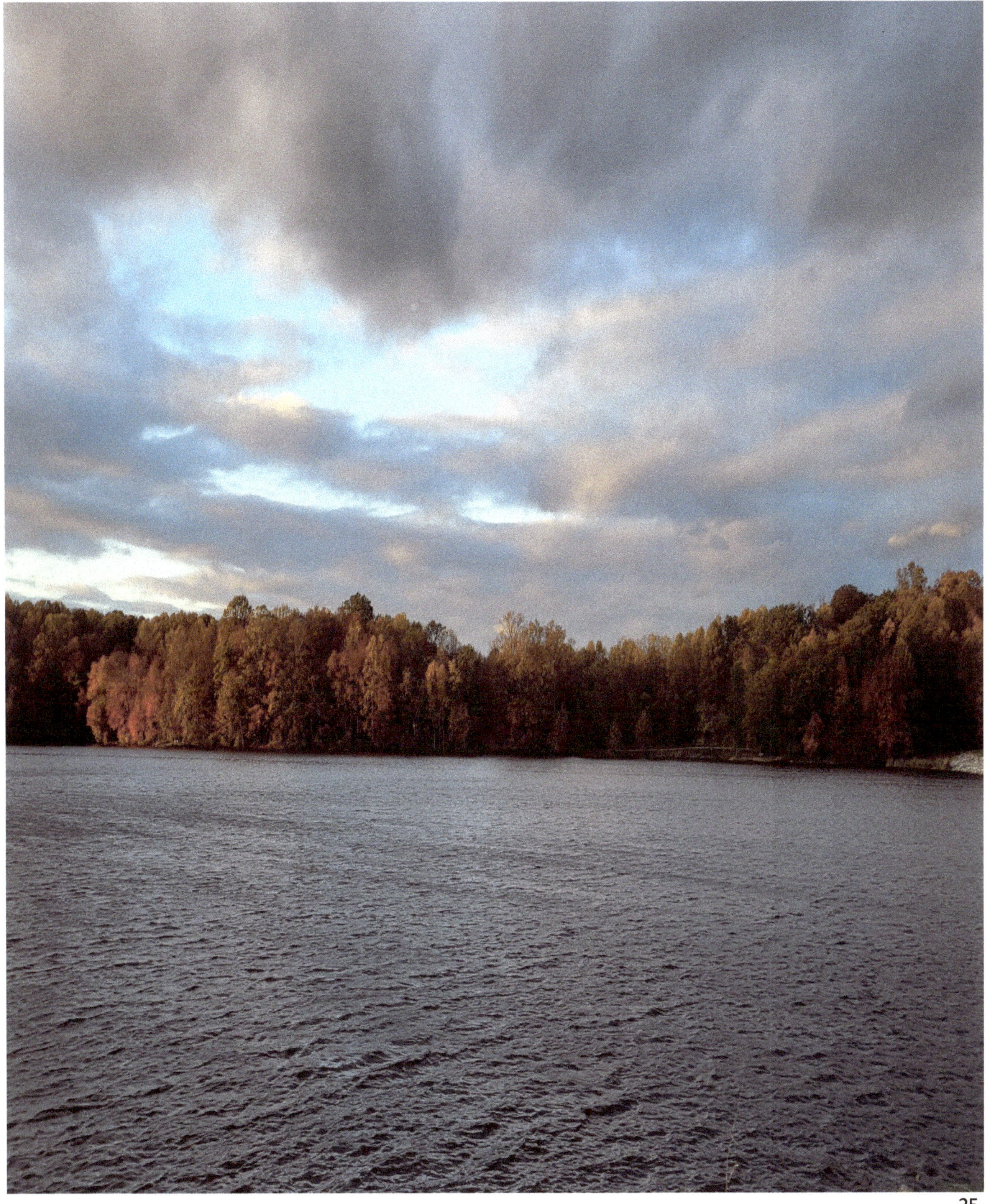

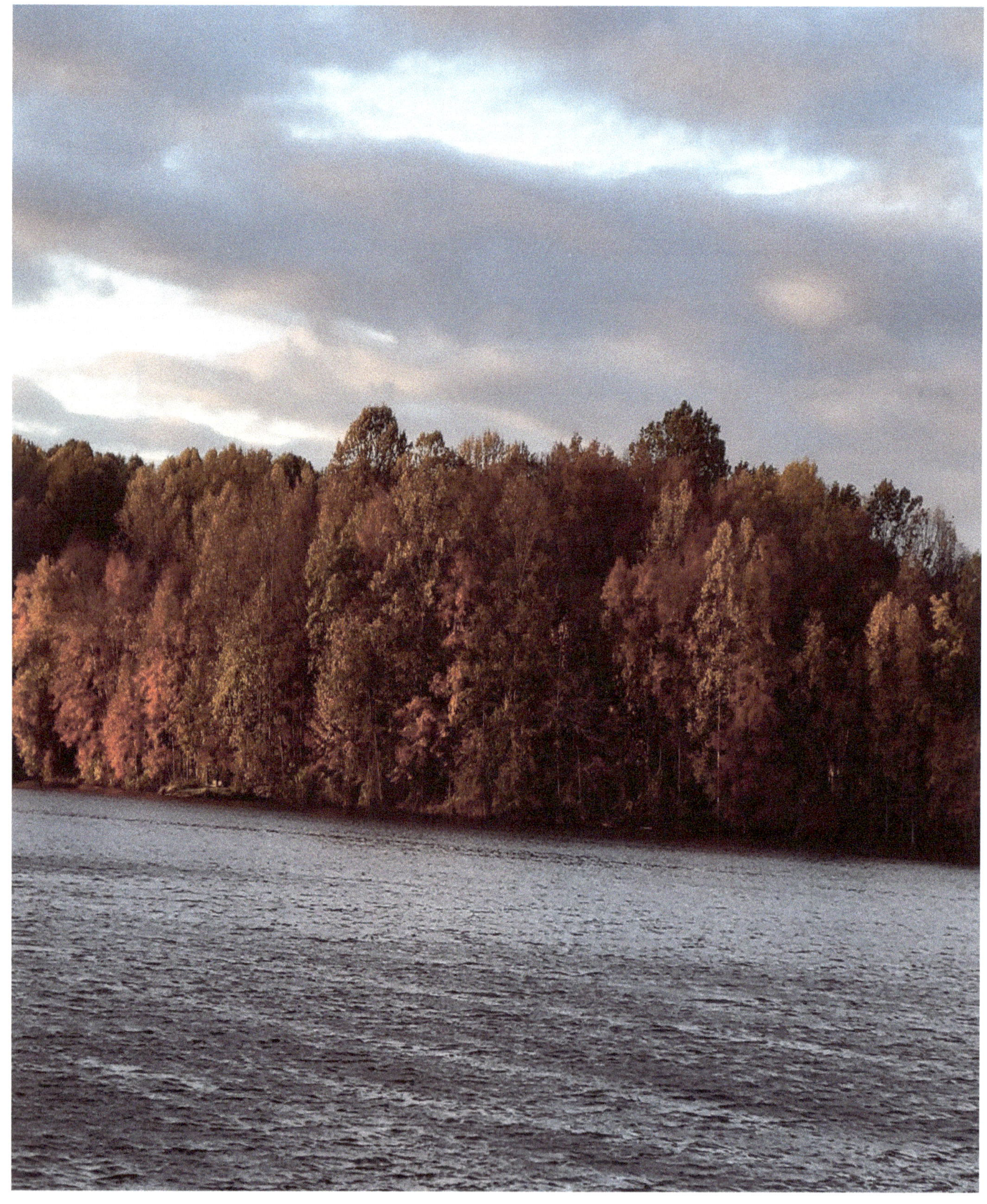

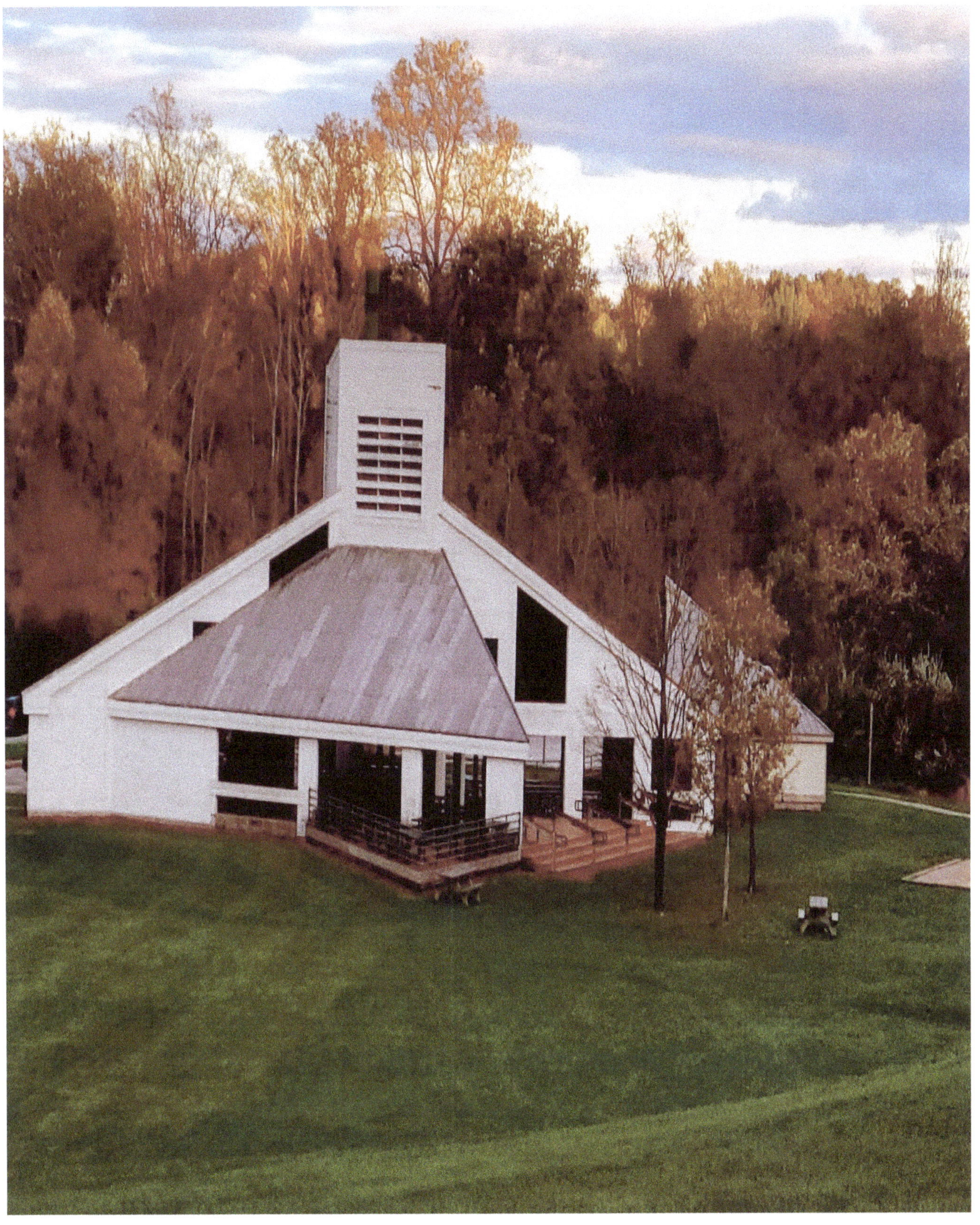

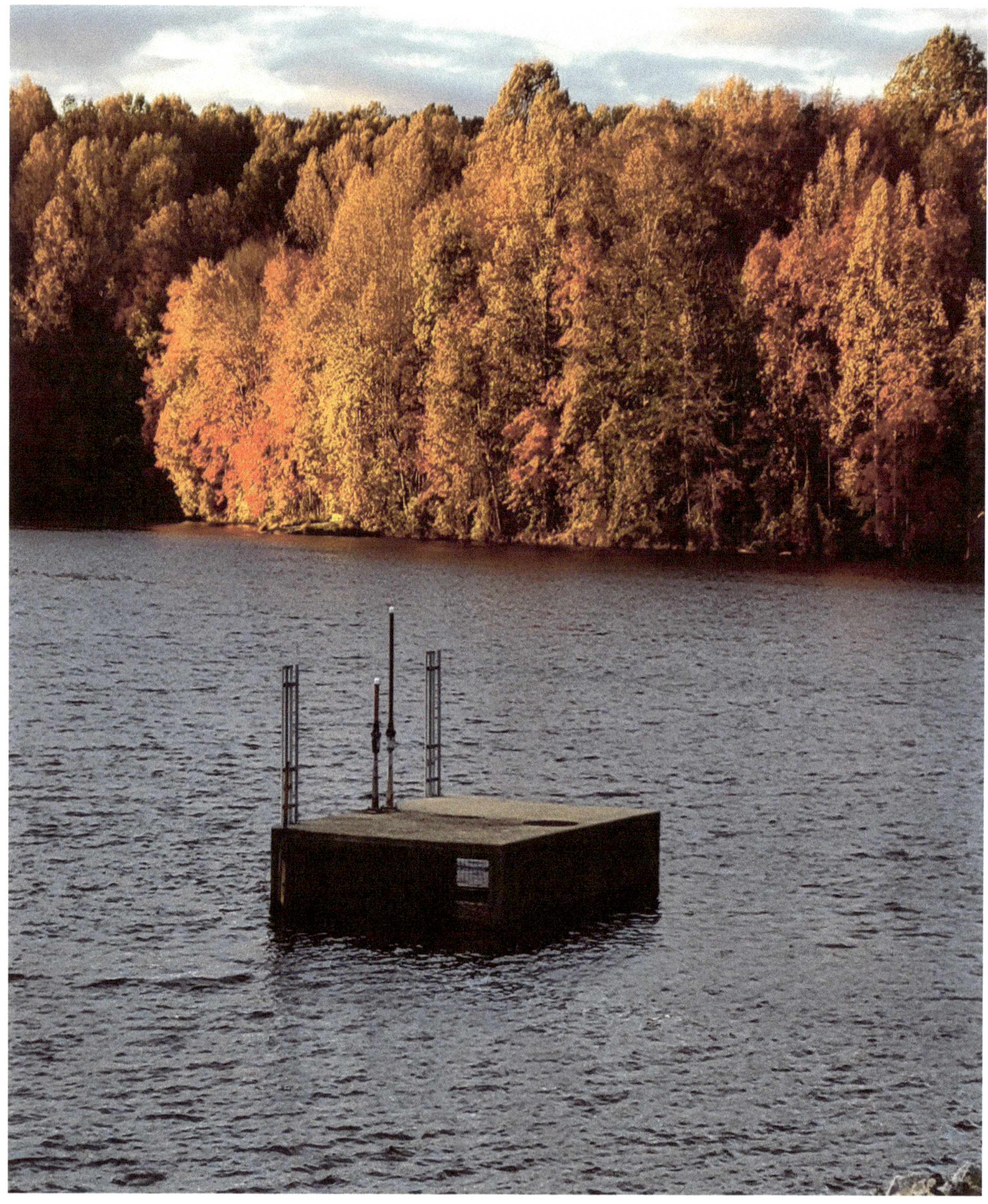

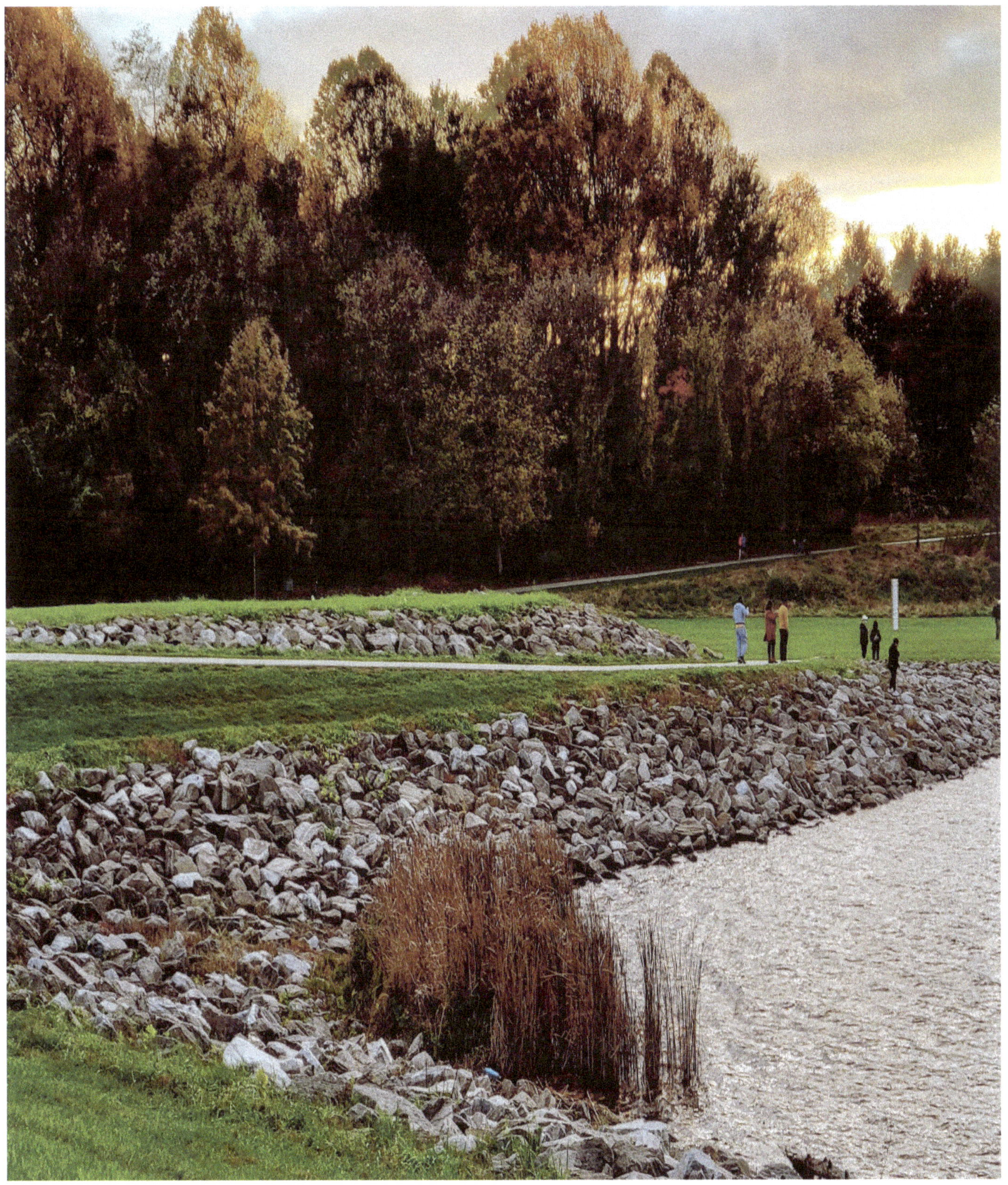

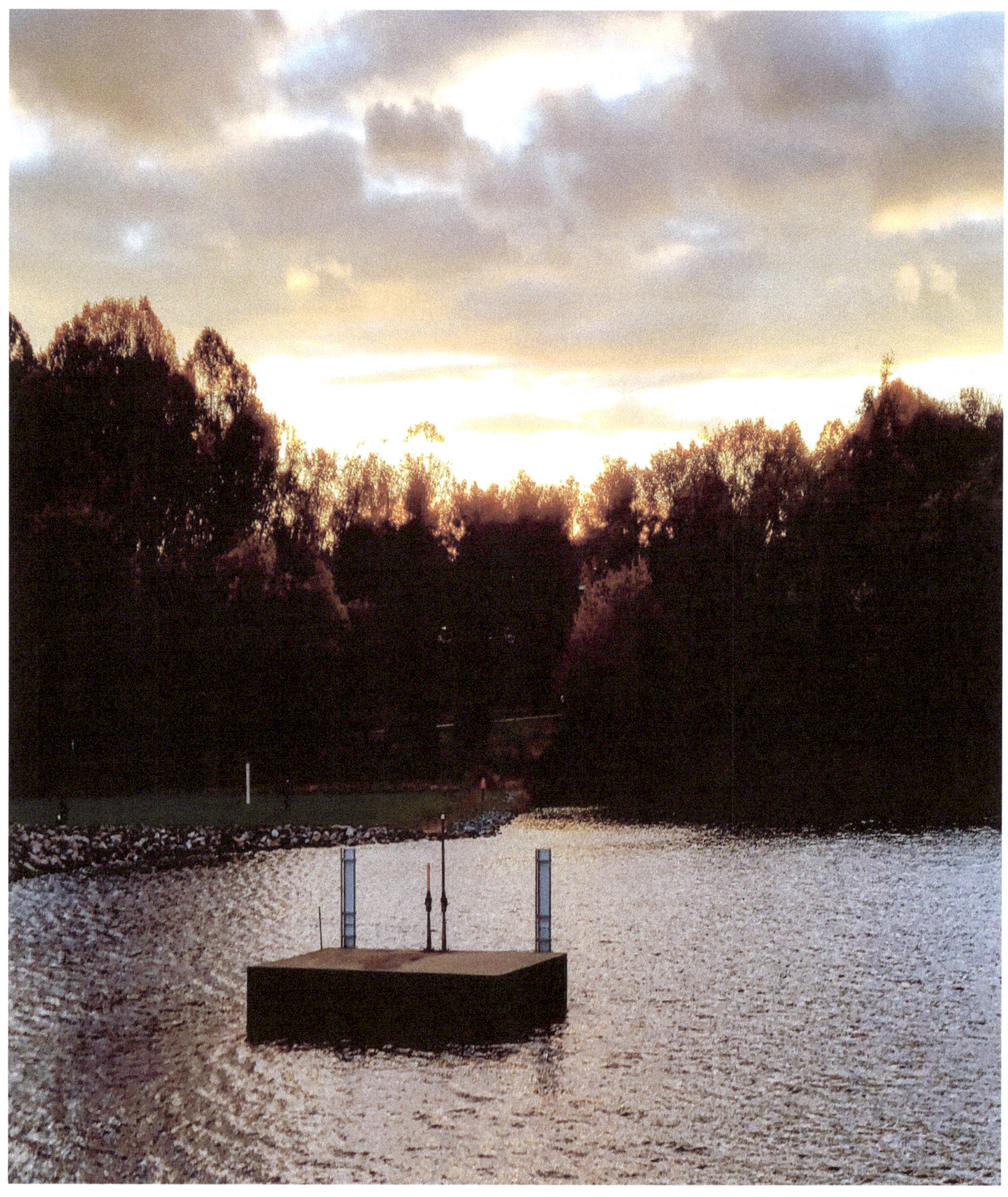

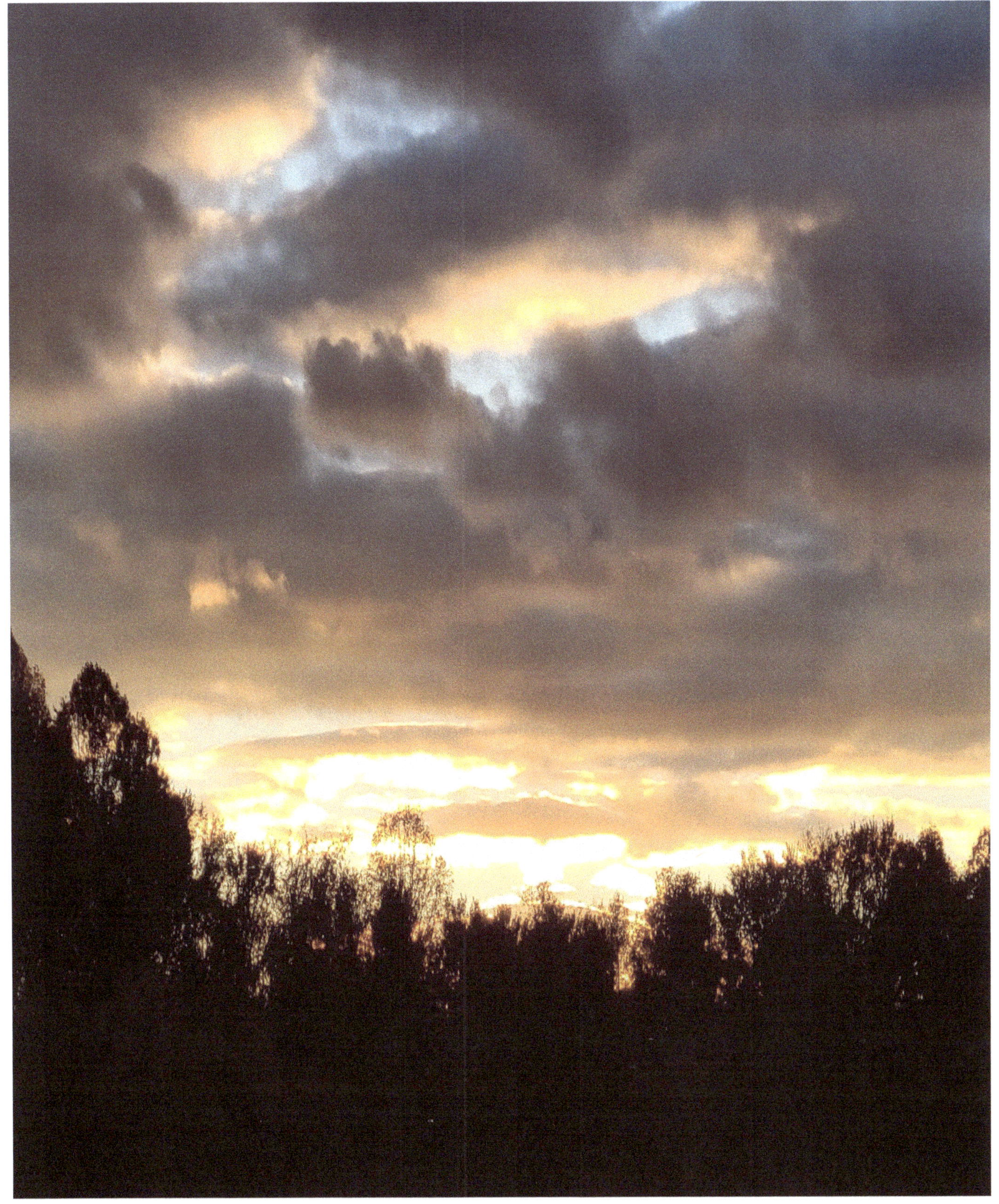

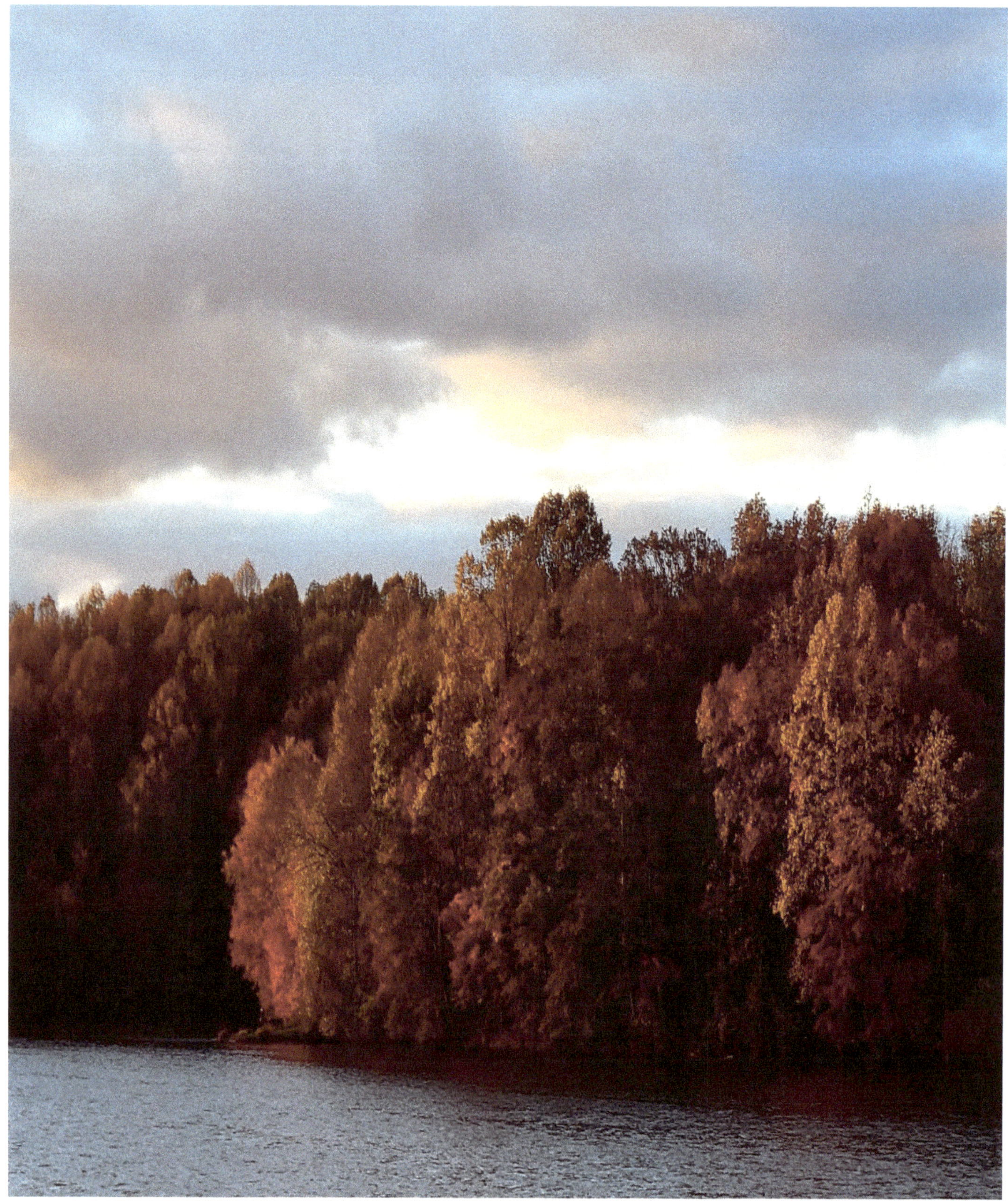

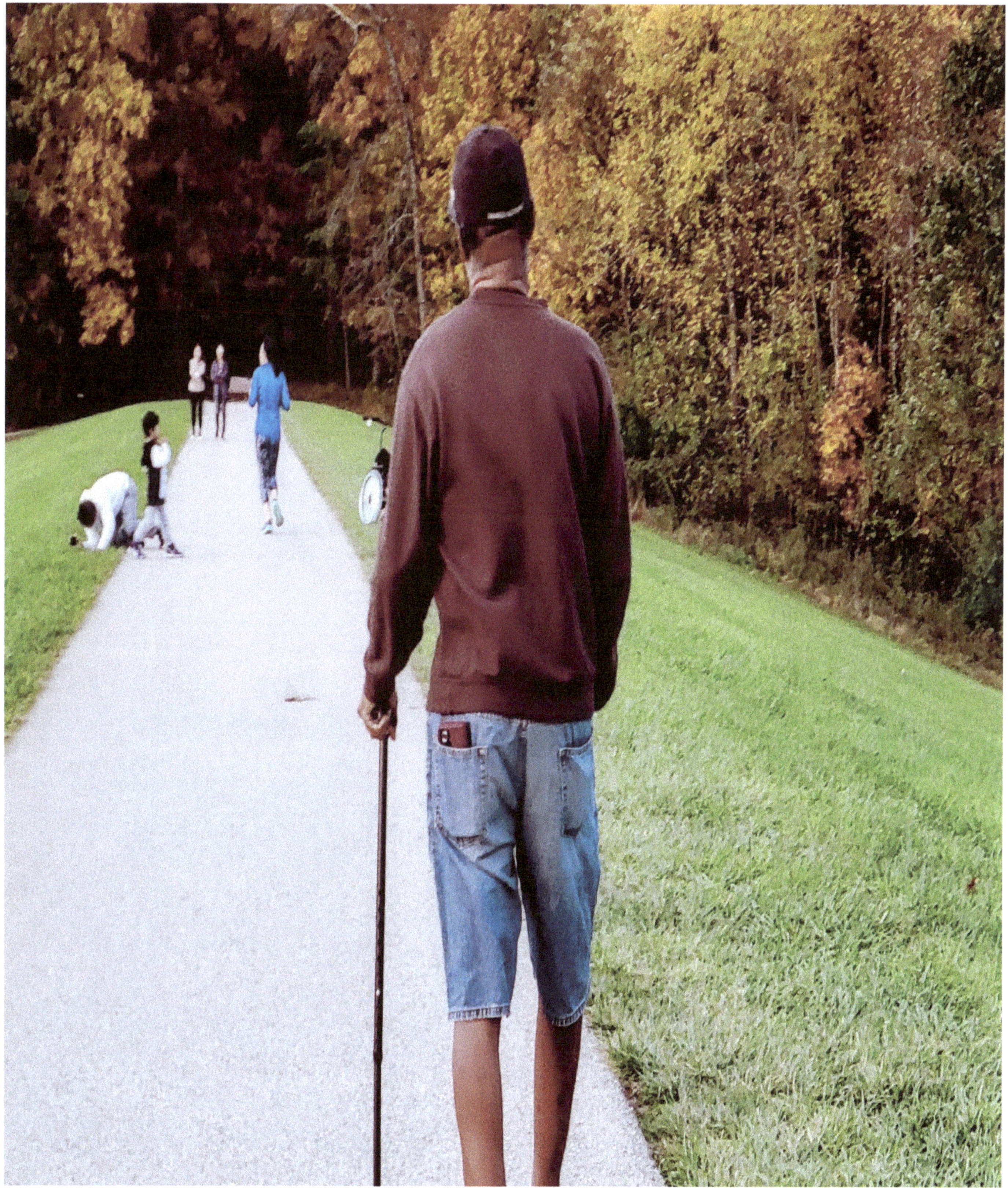

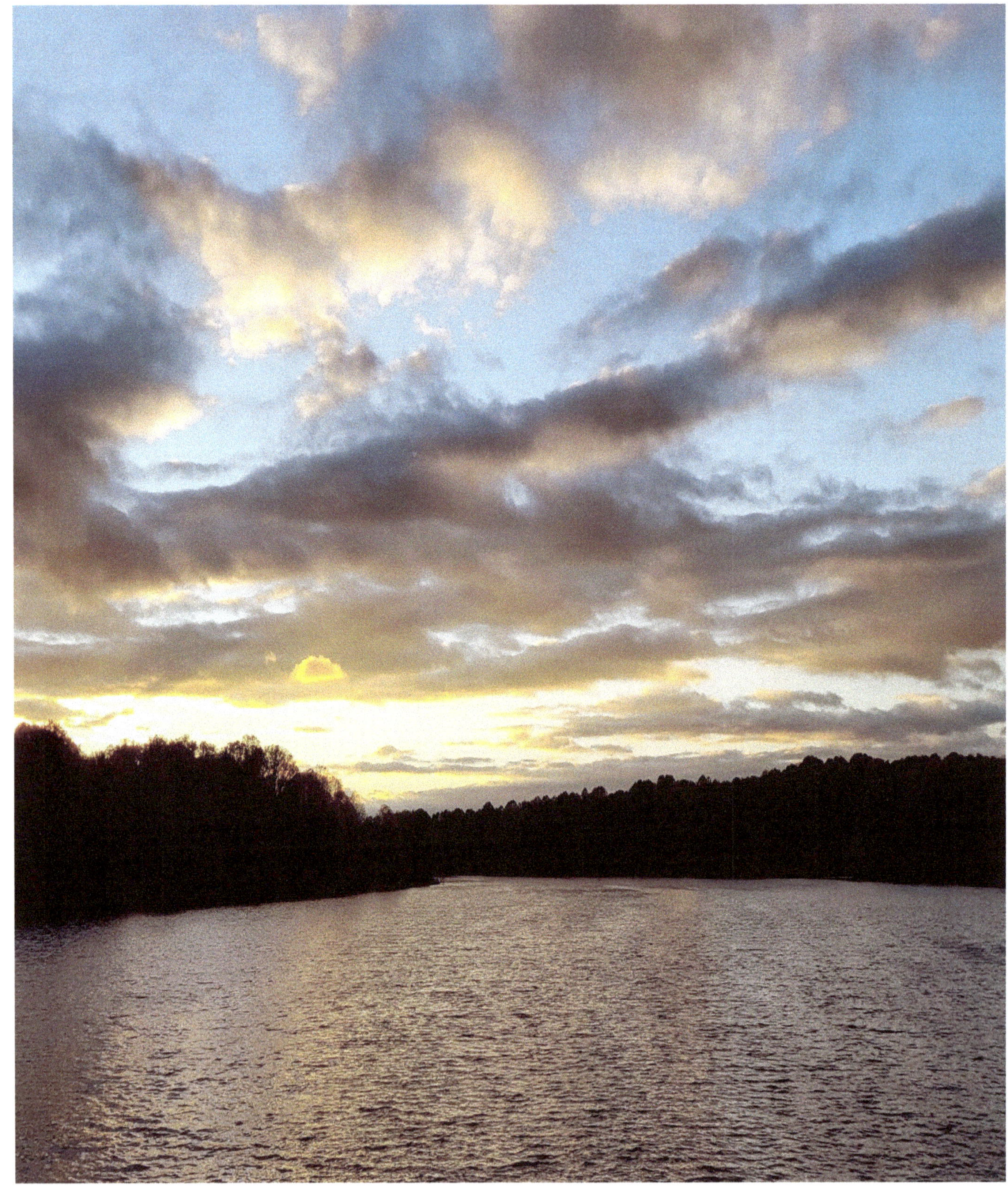

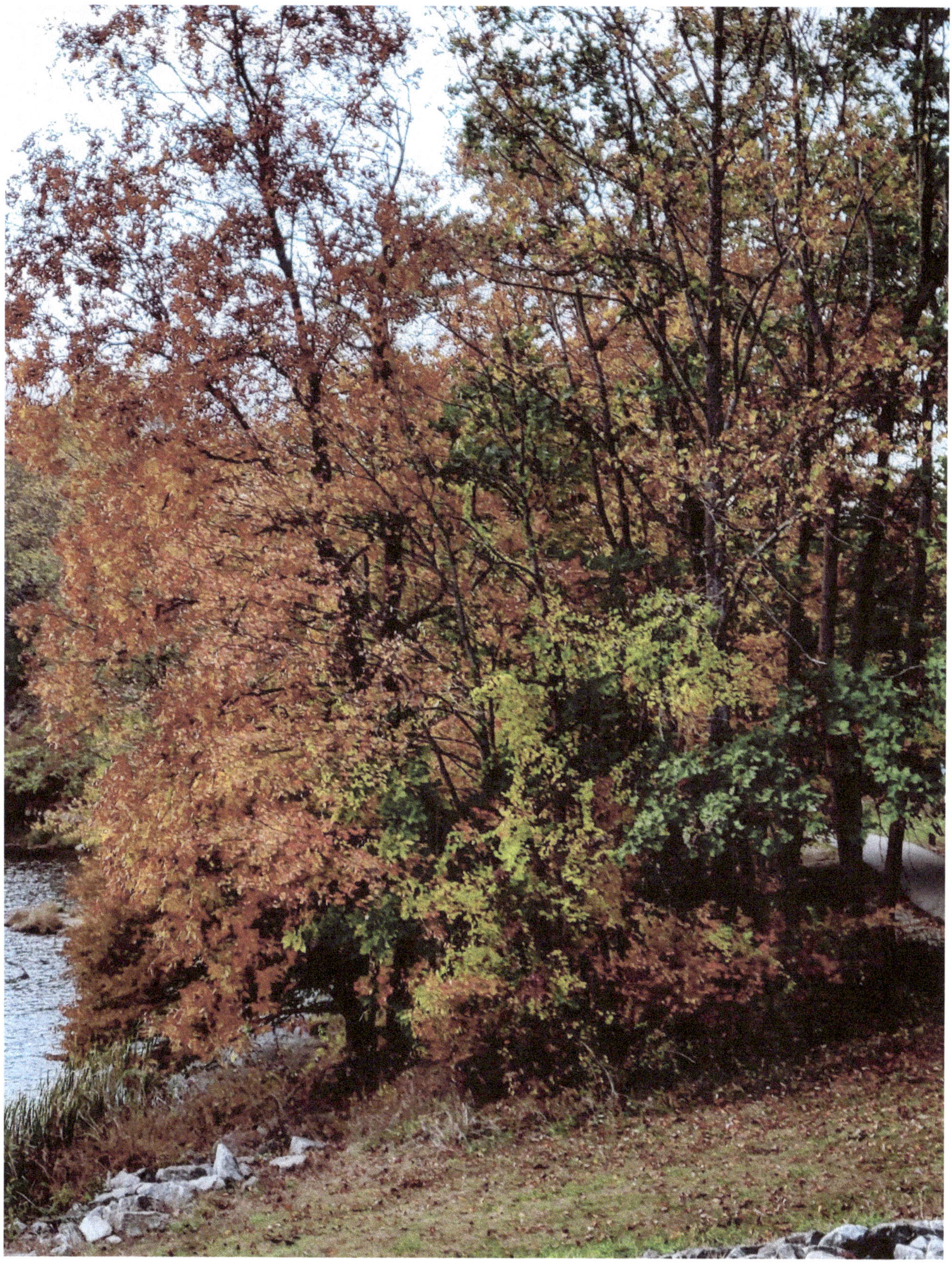

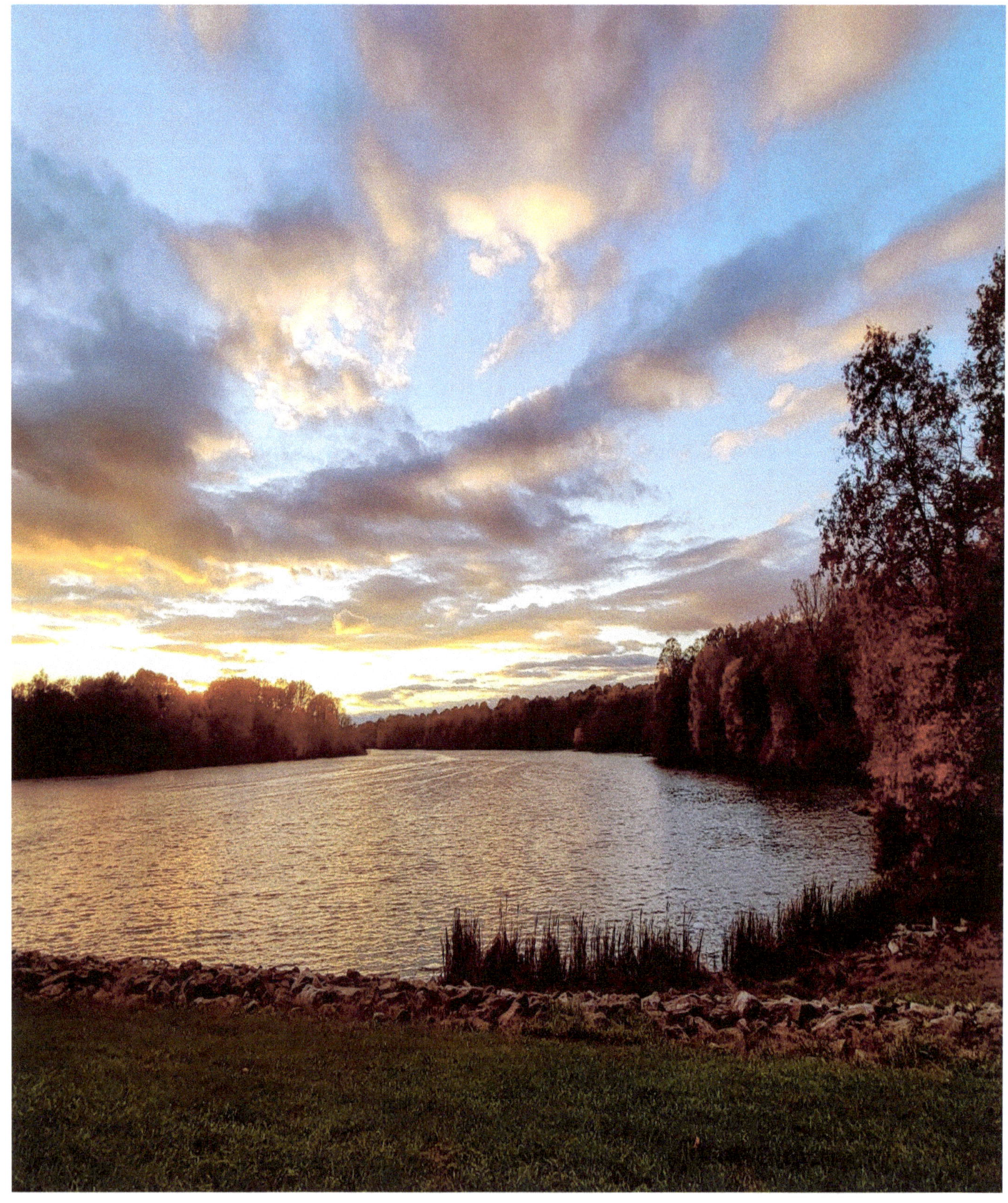

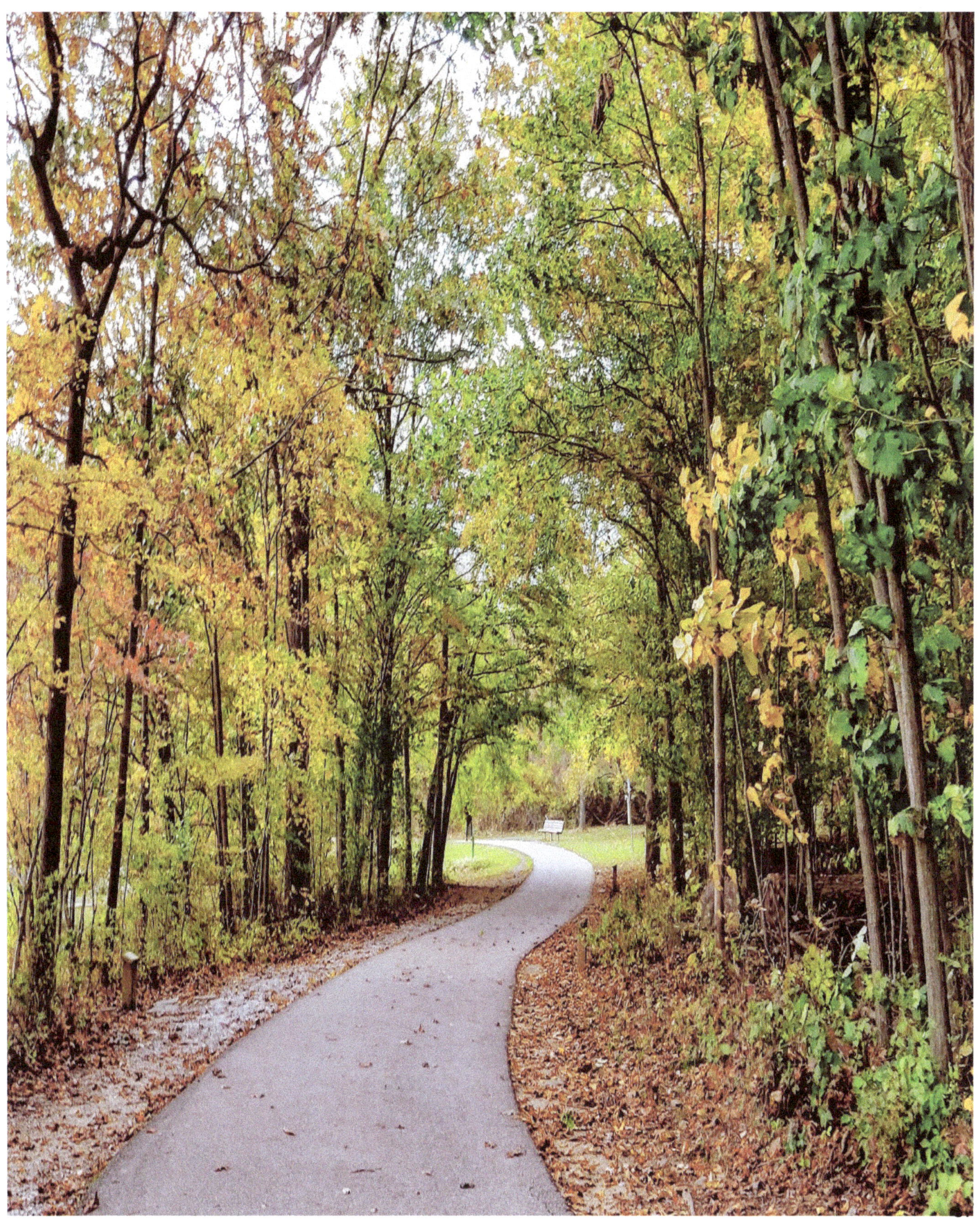

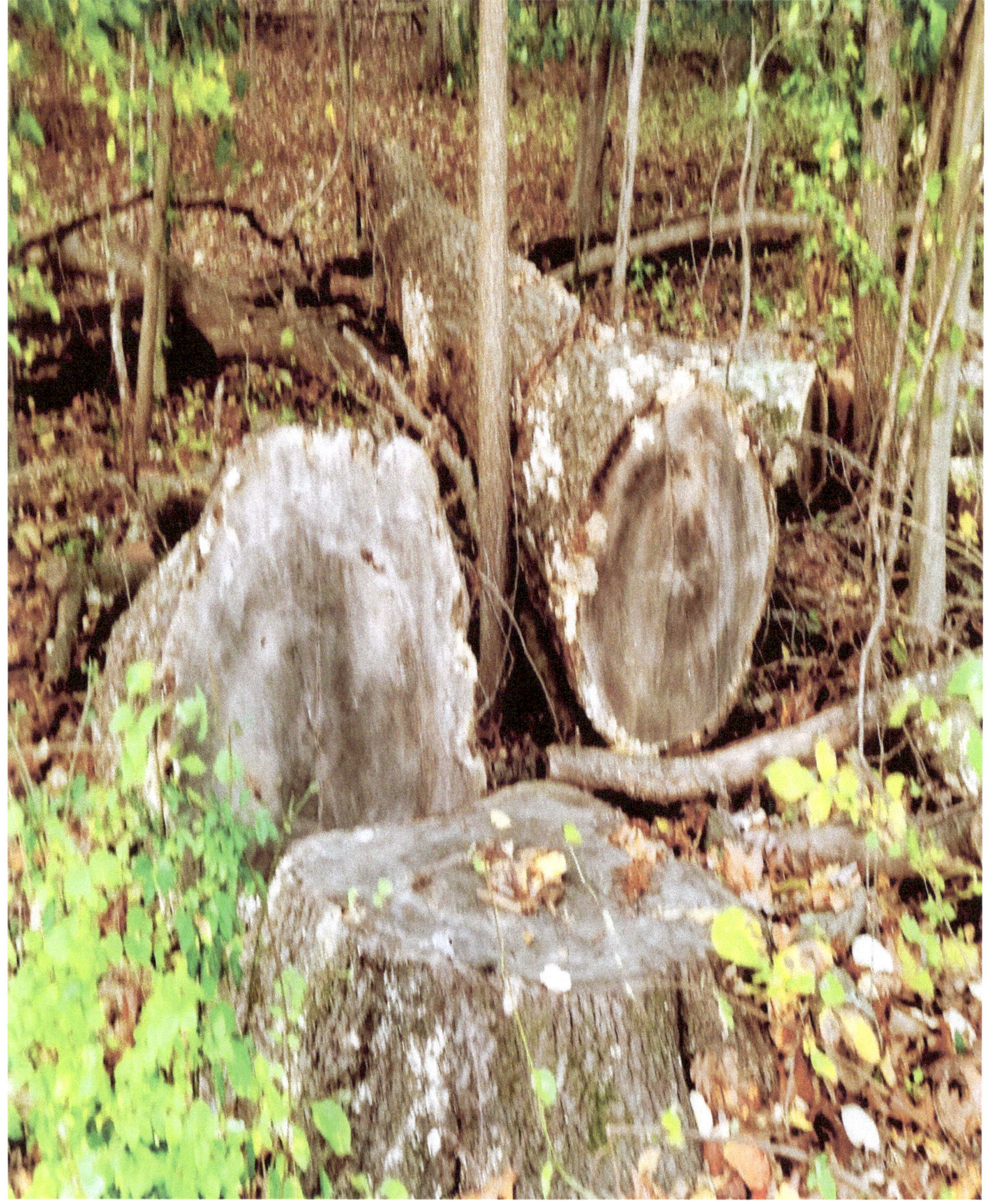

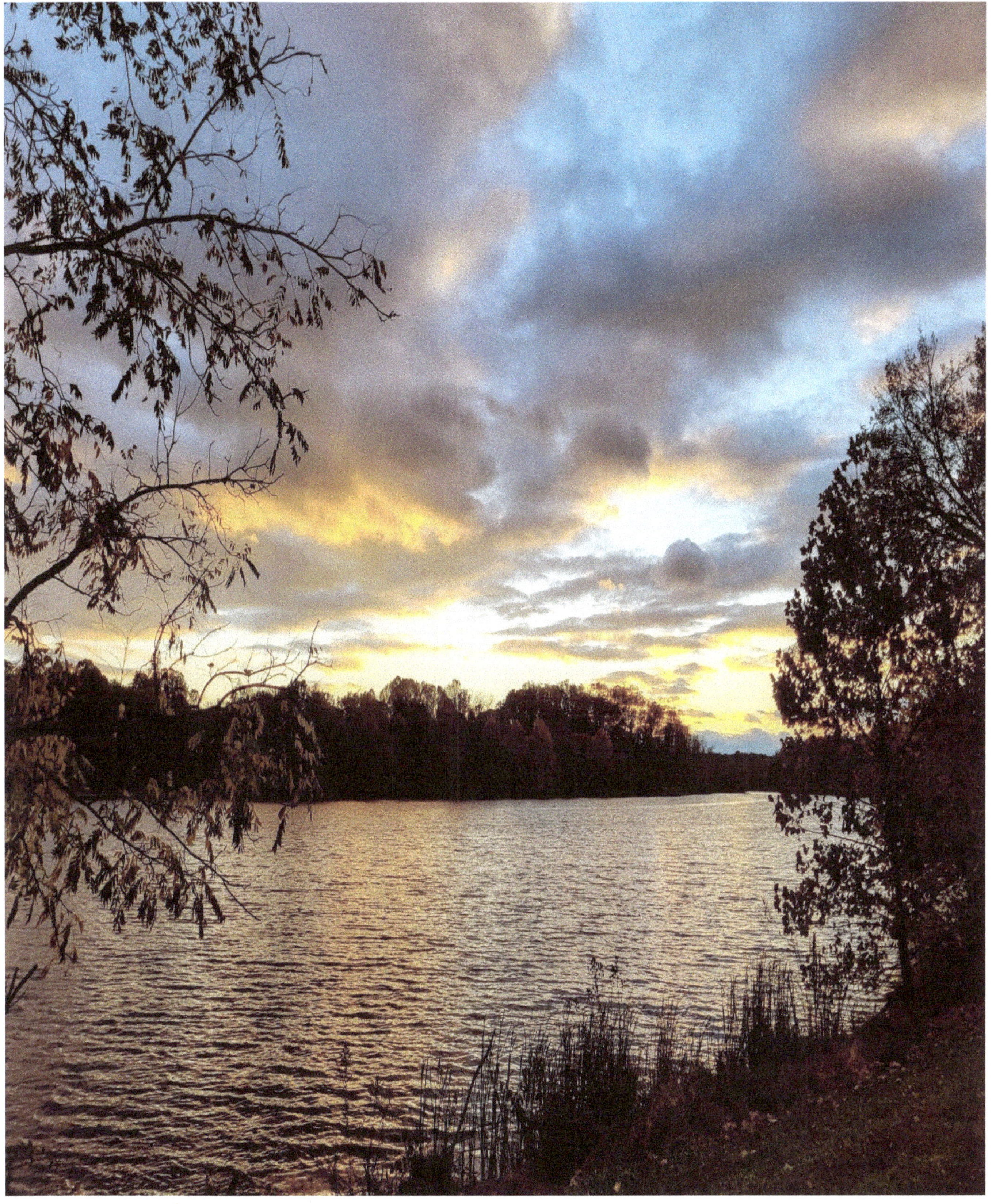

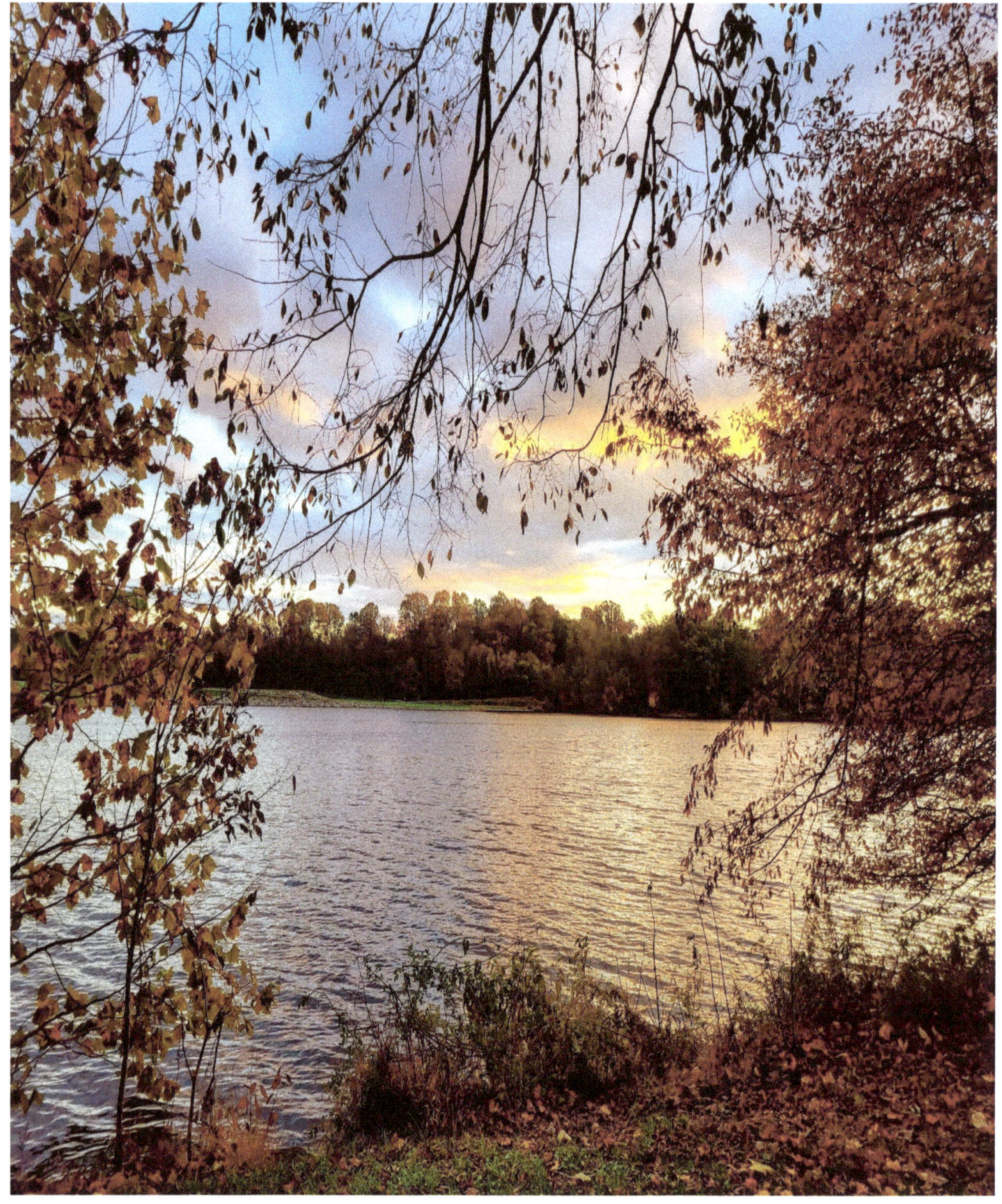

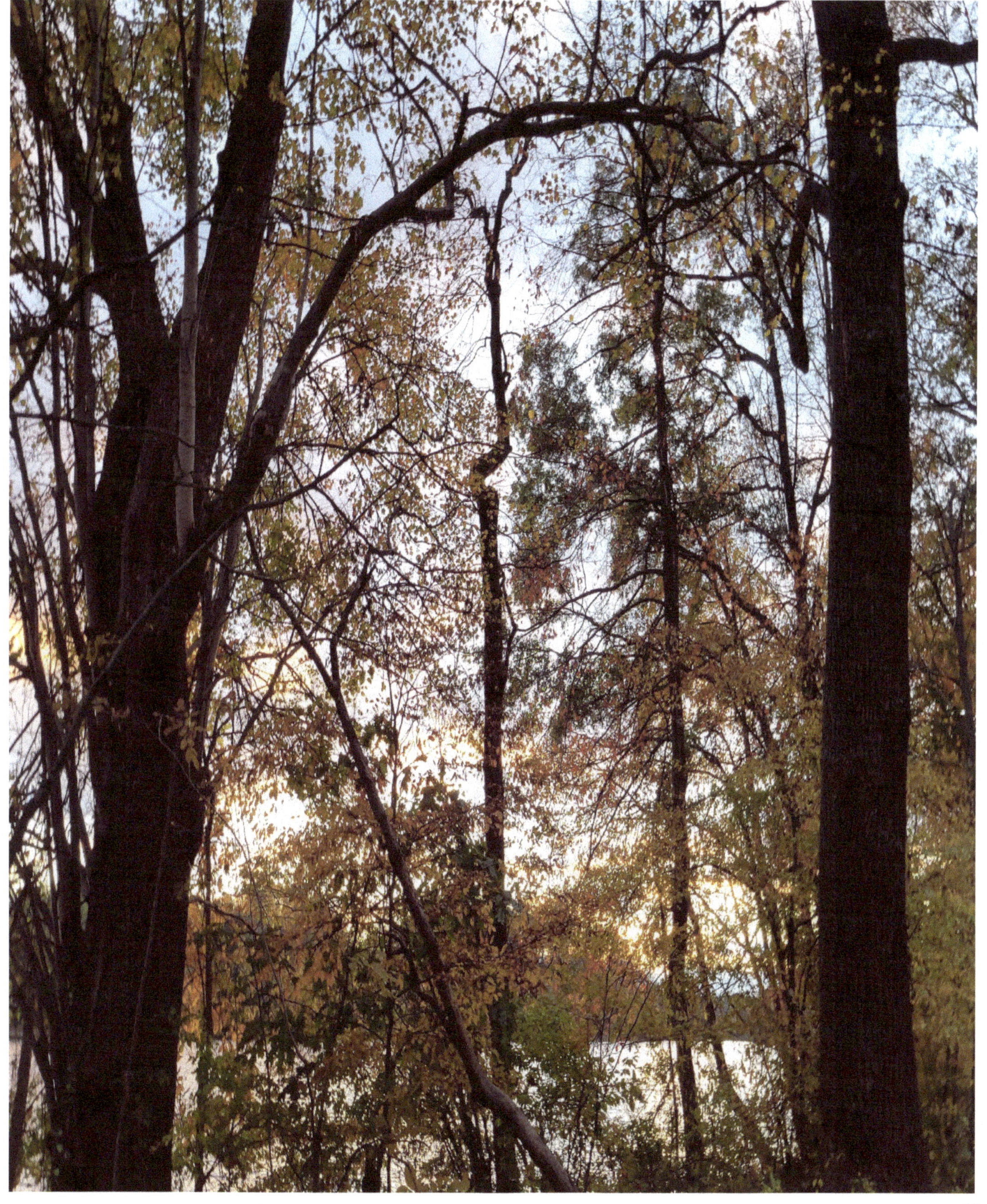

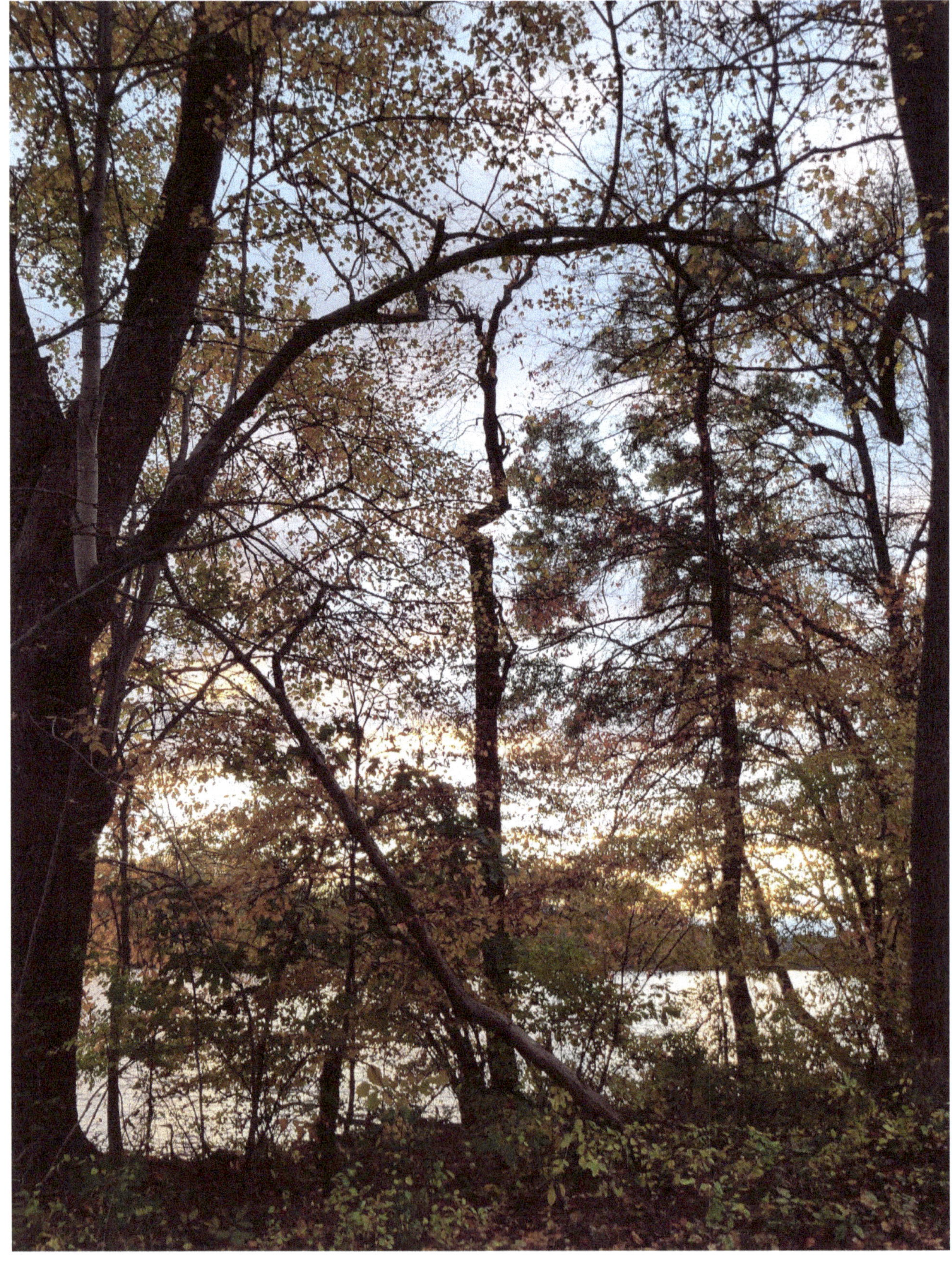

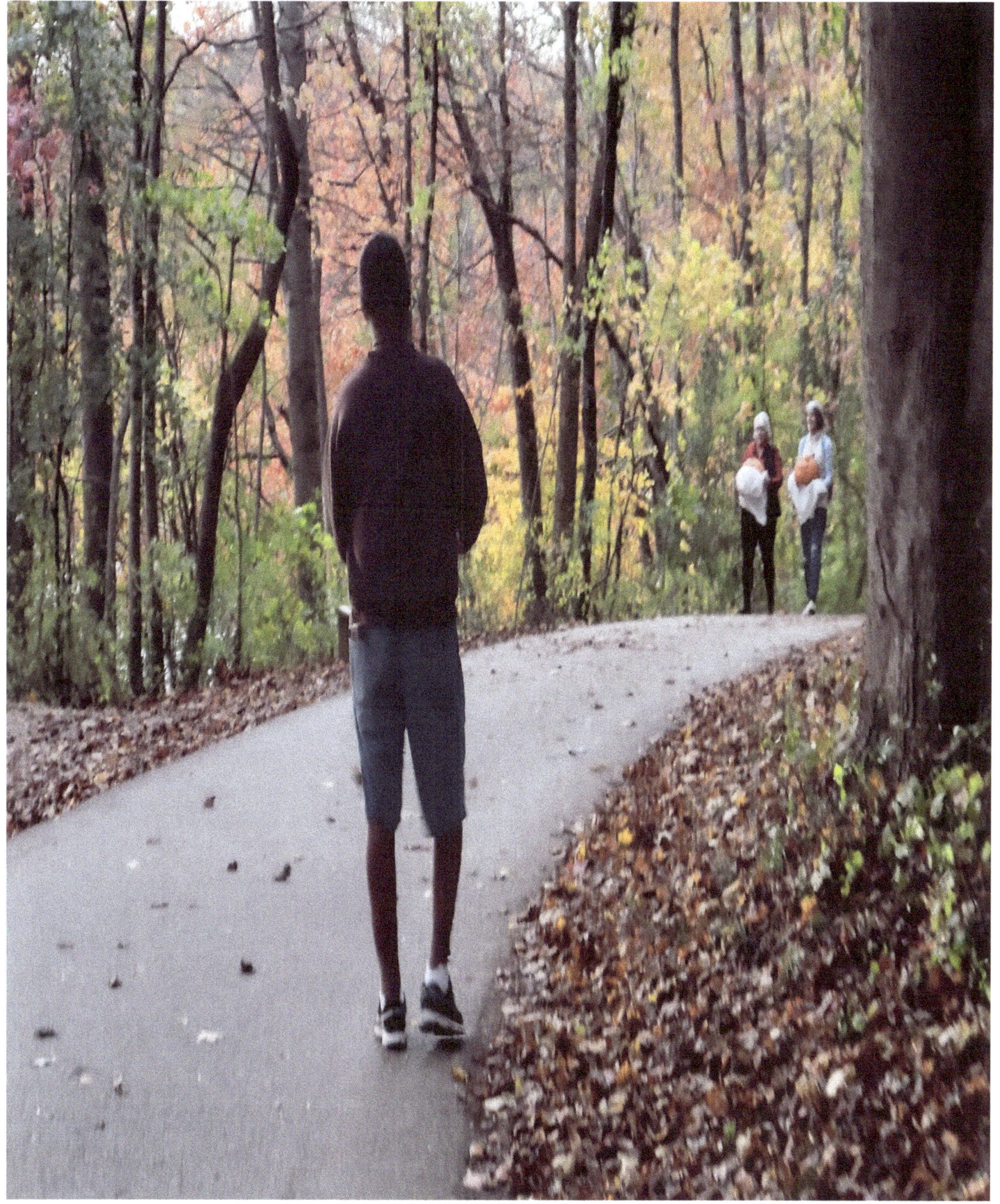

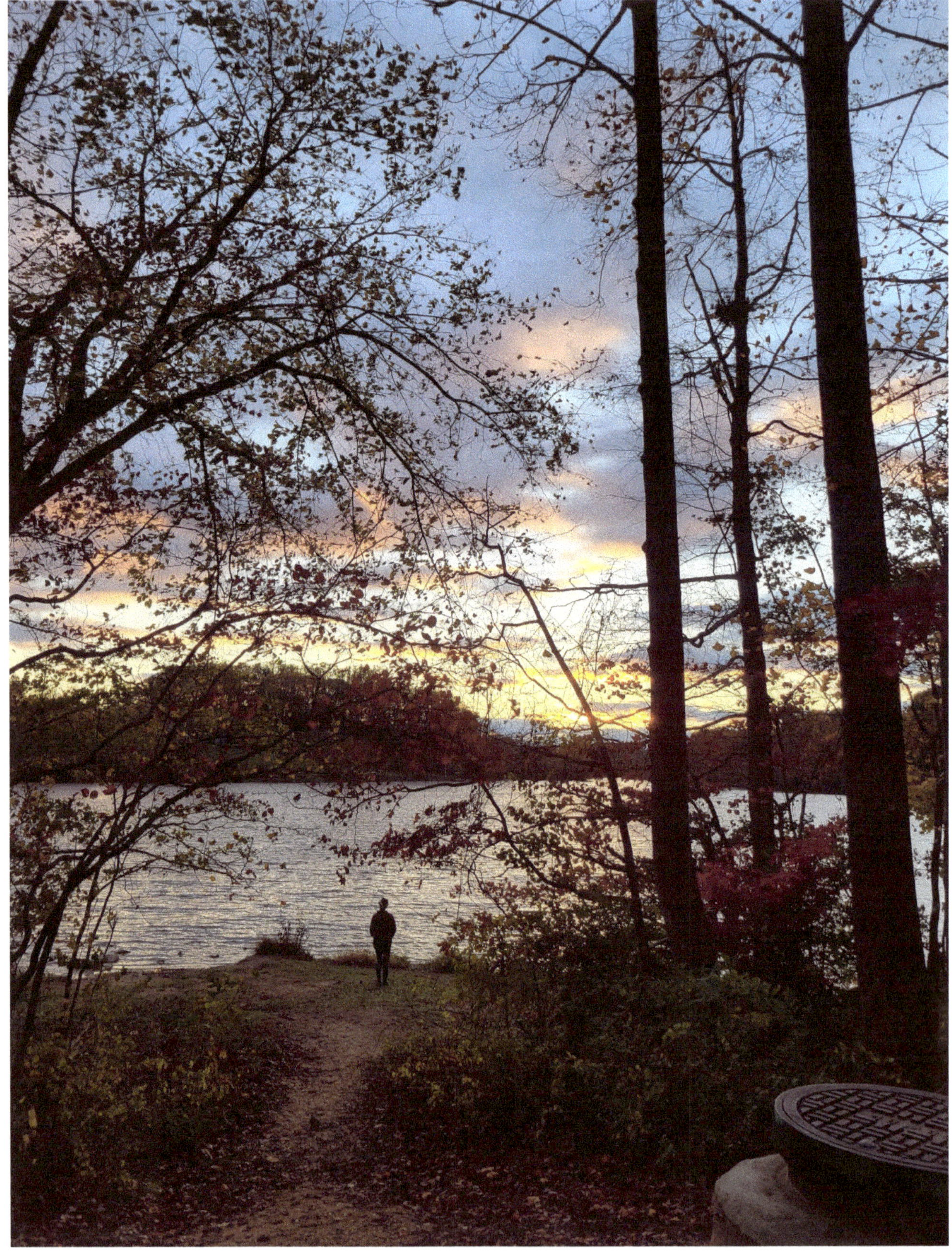

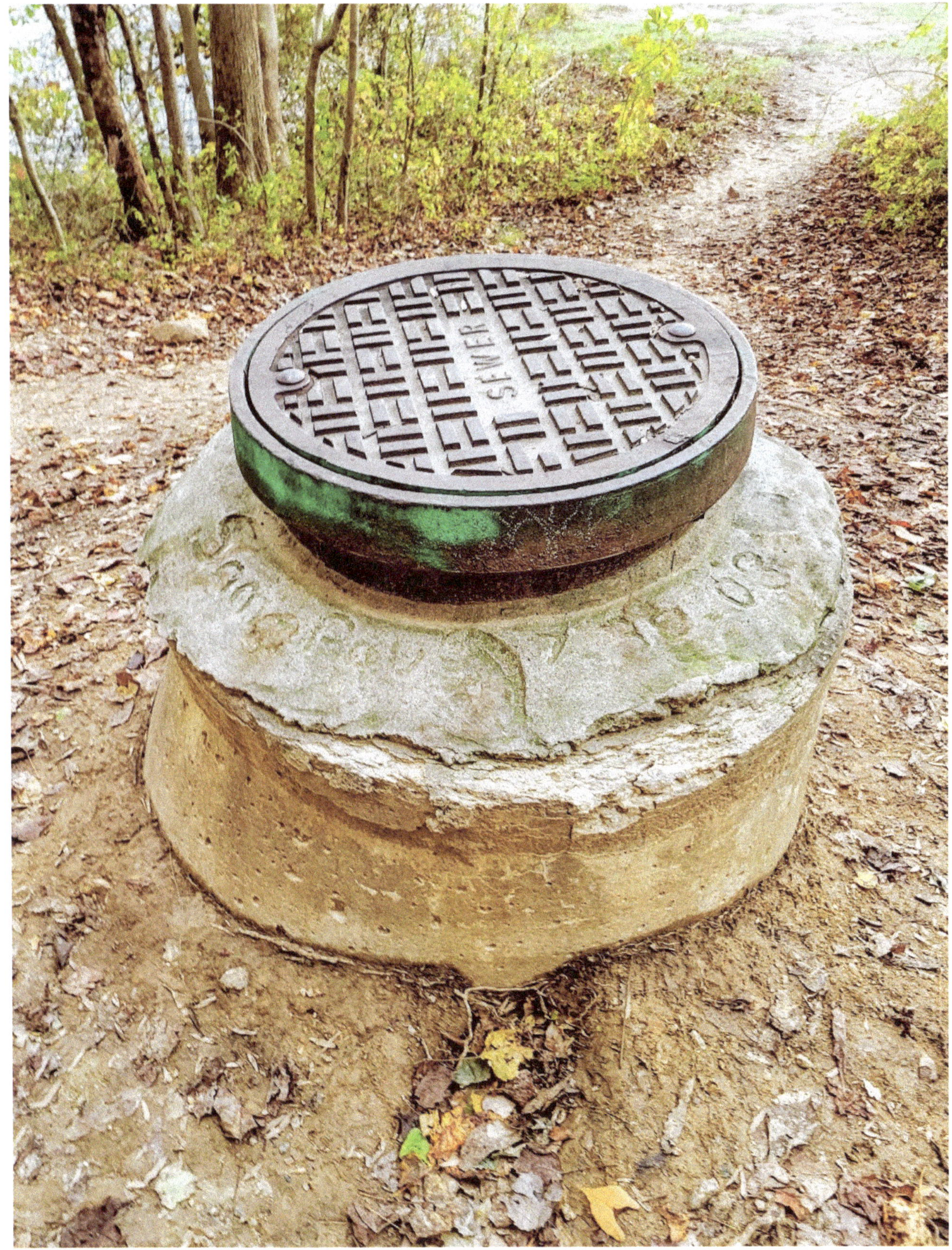

SEWER

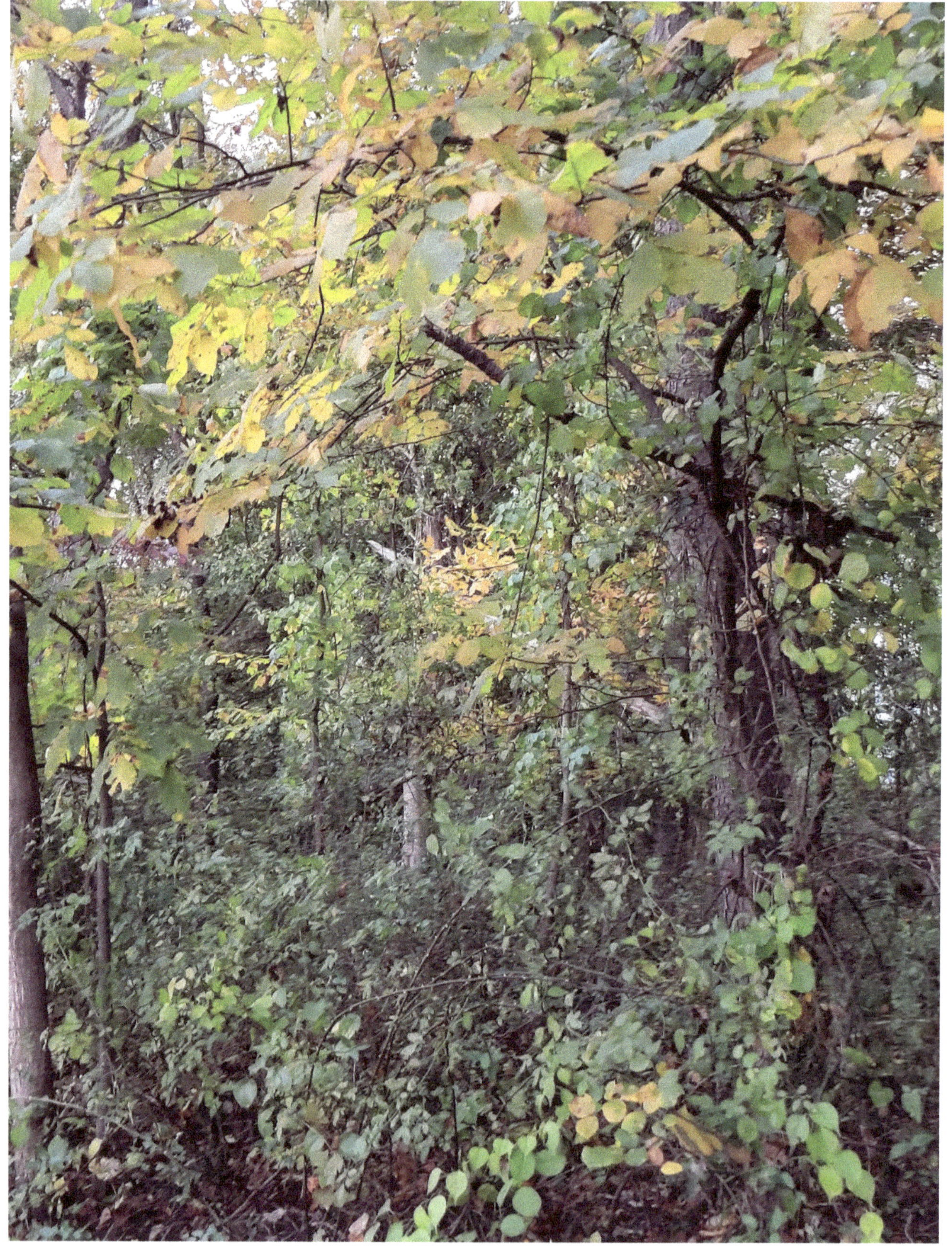

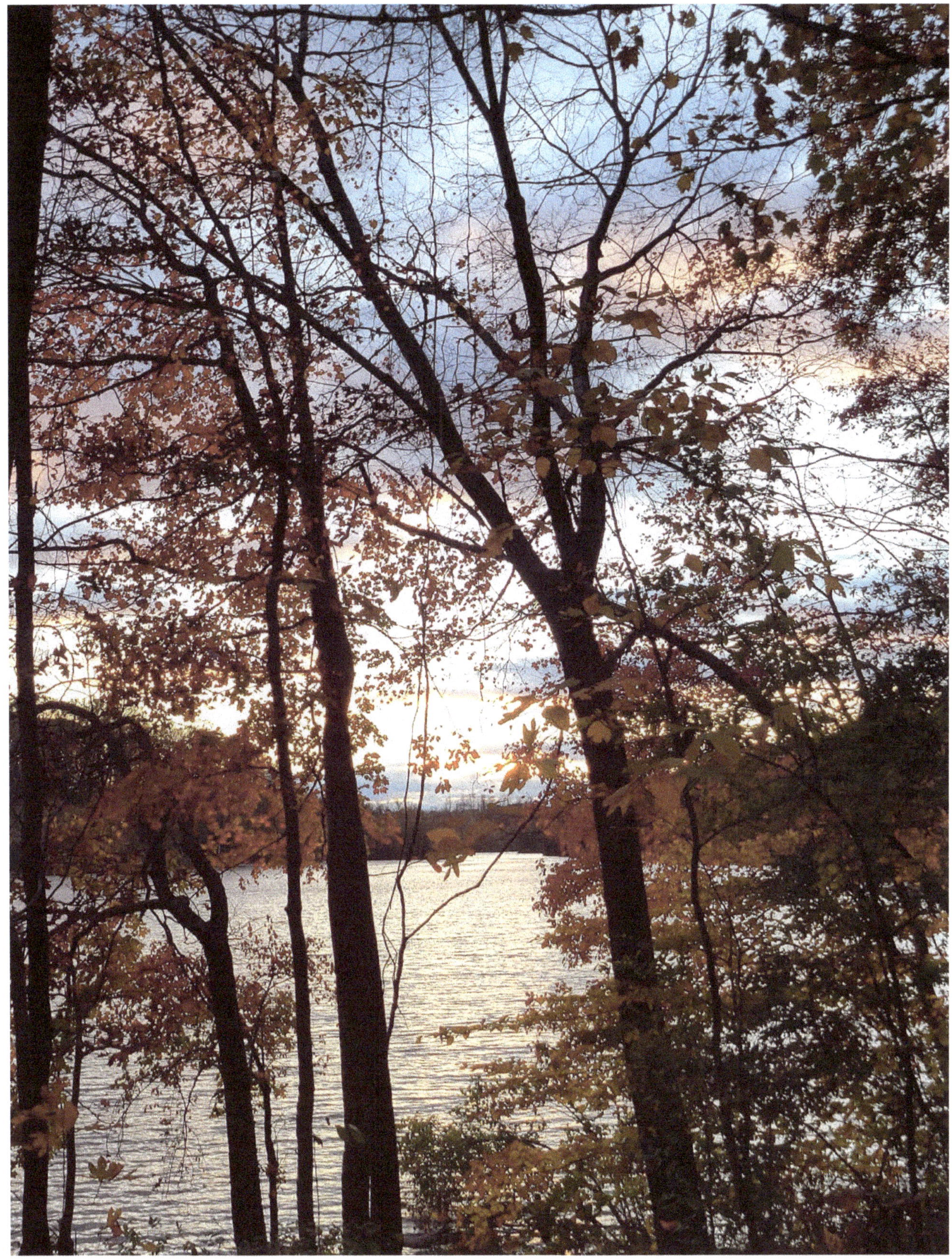

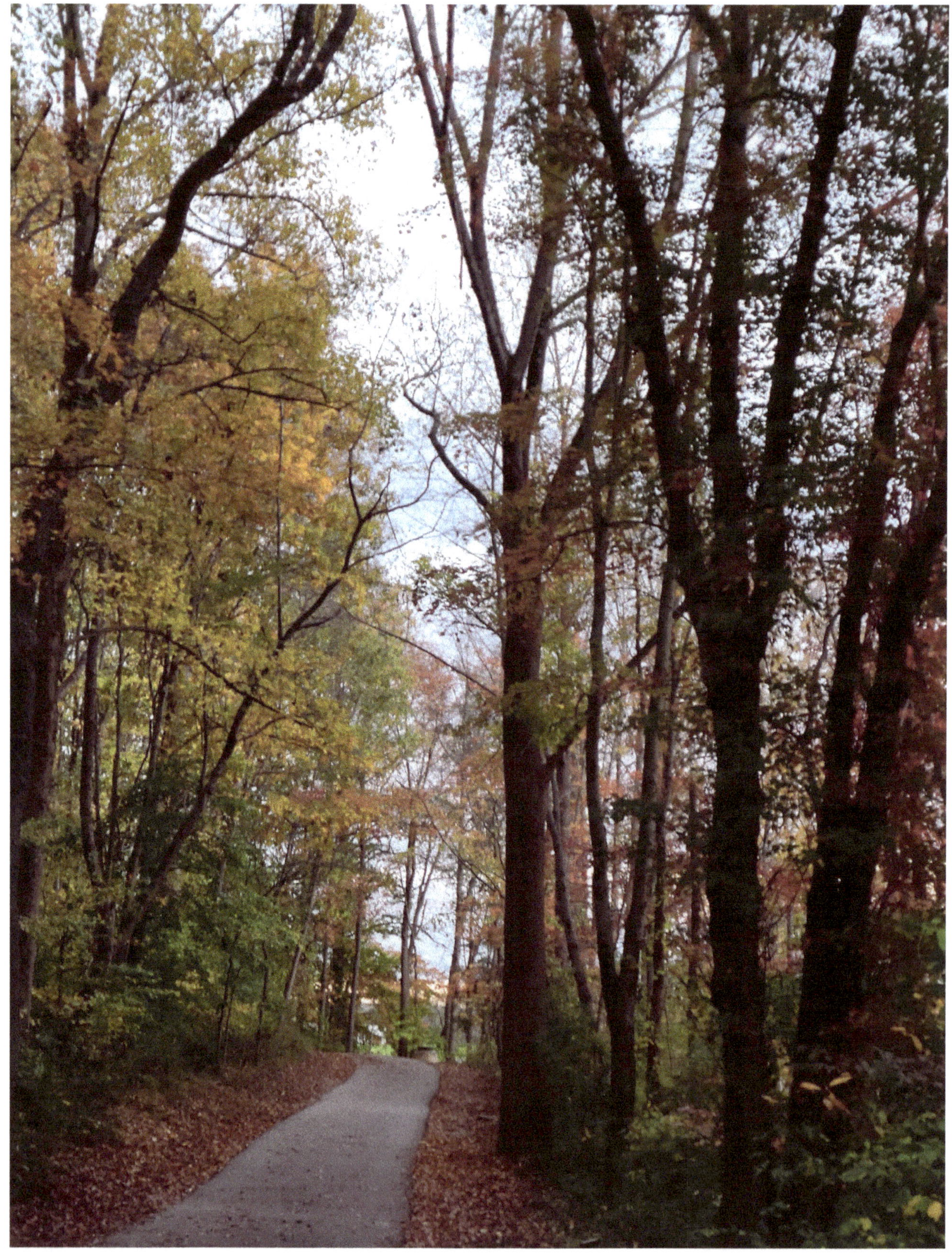

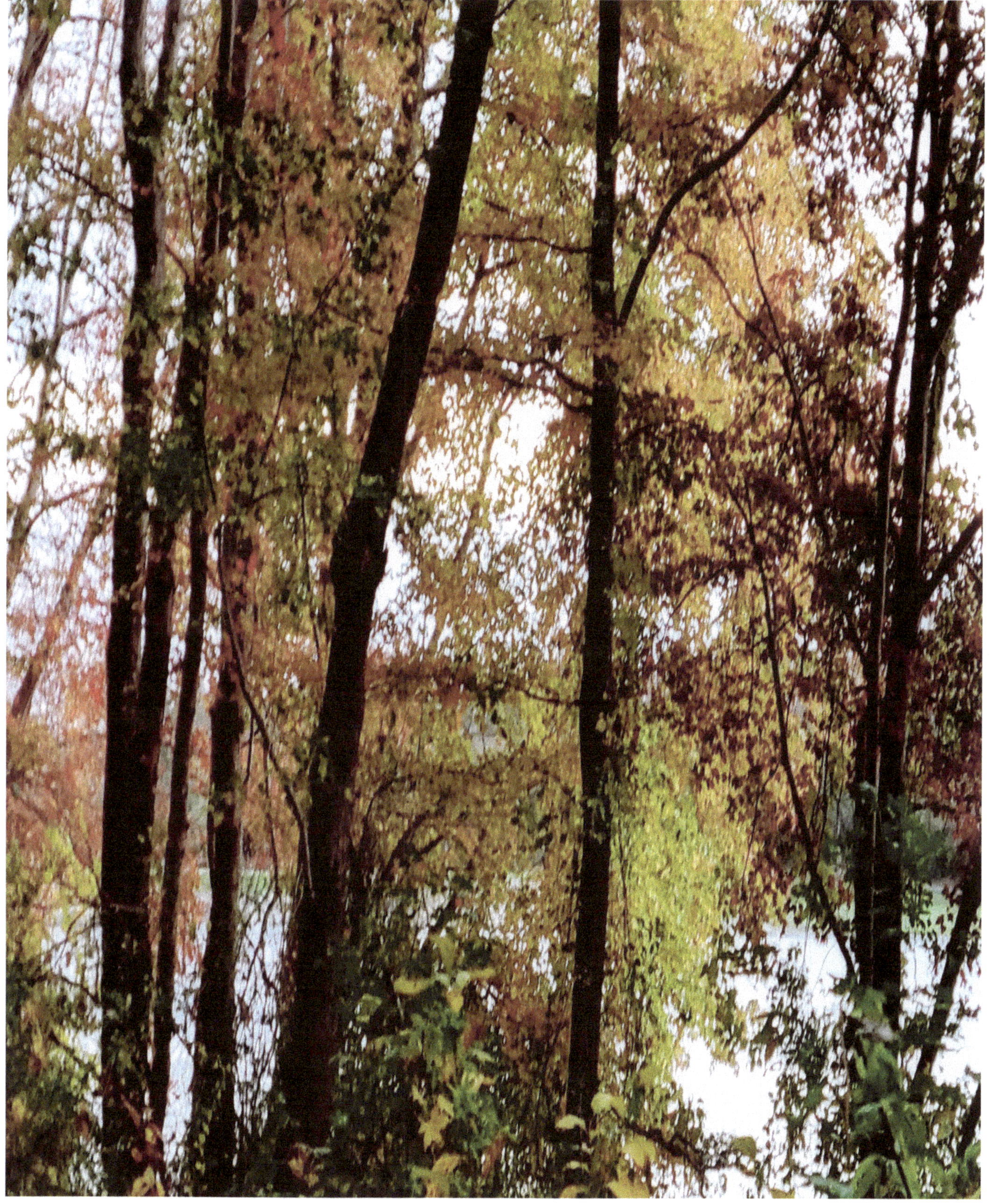

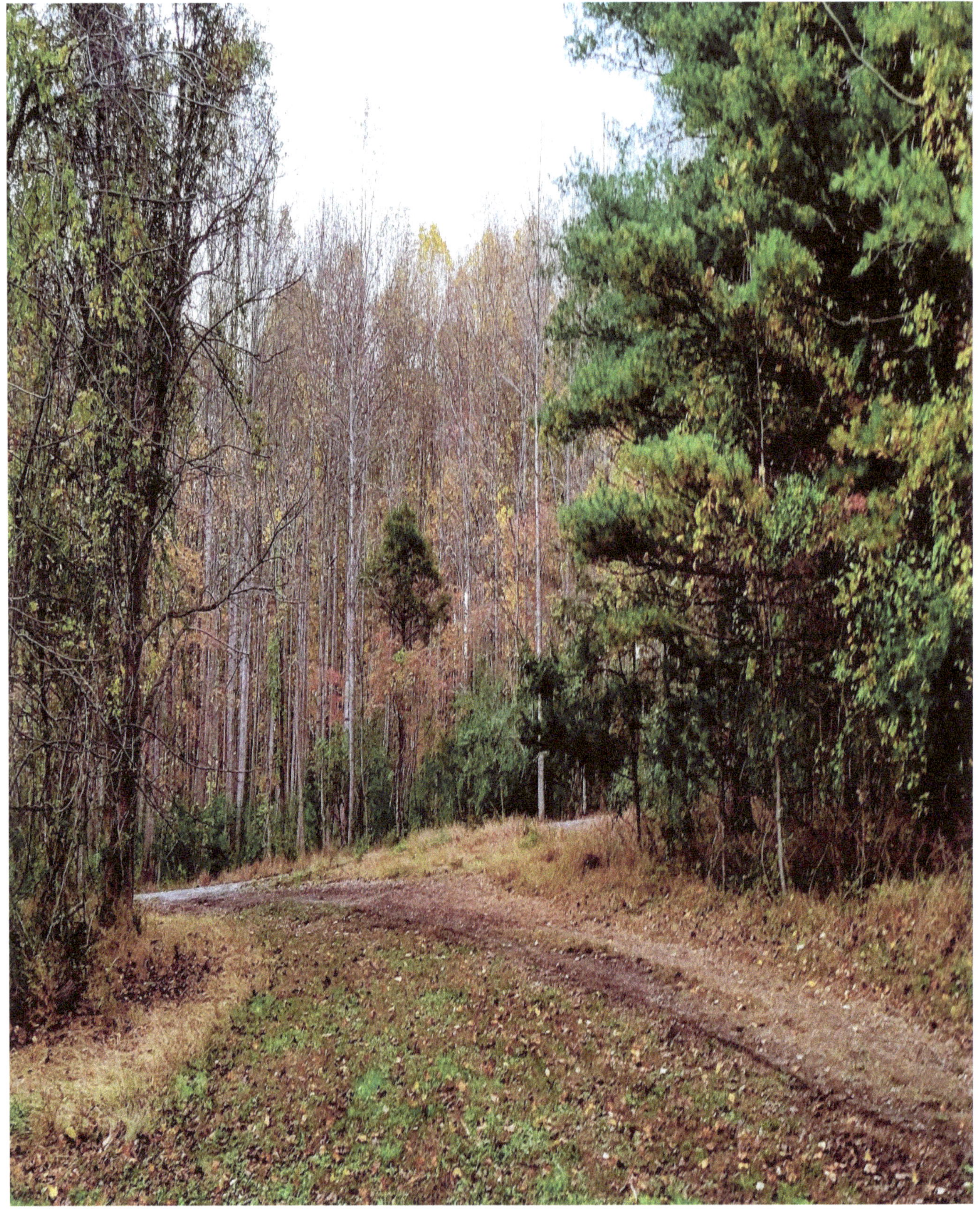

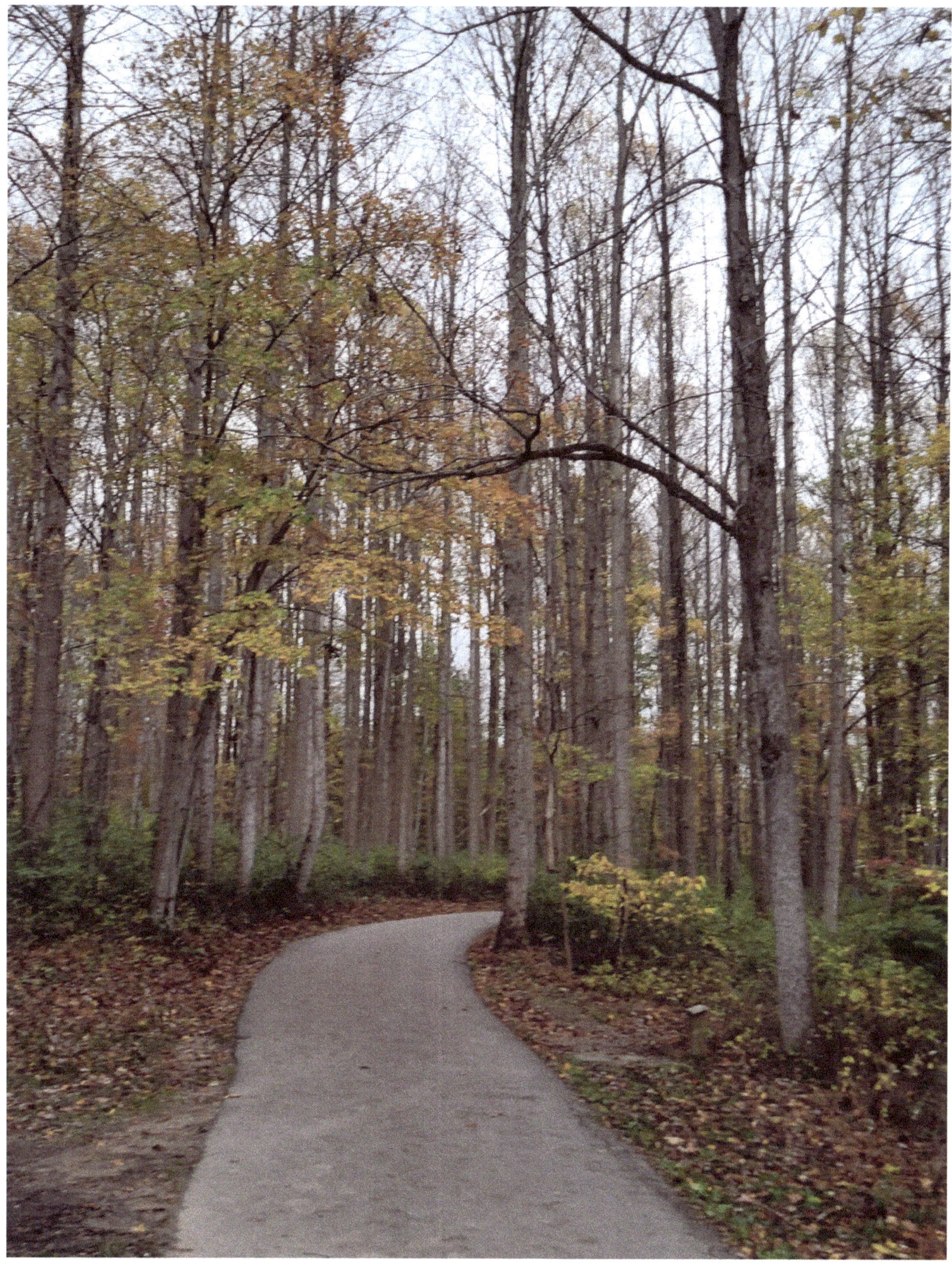

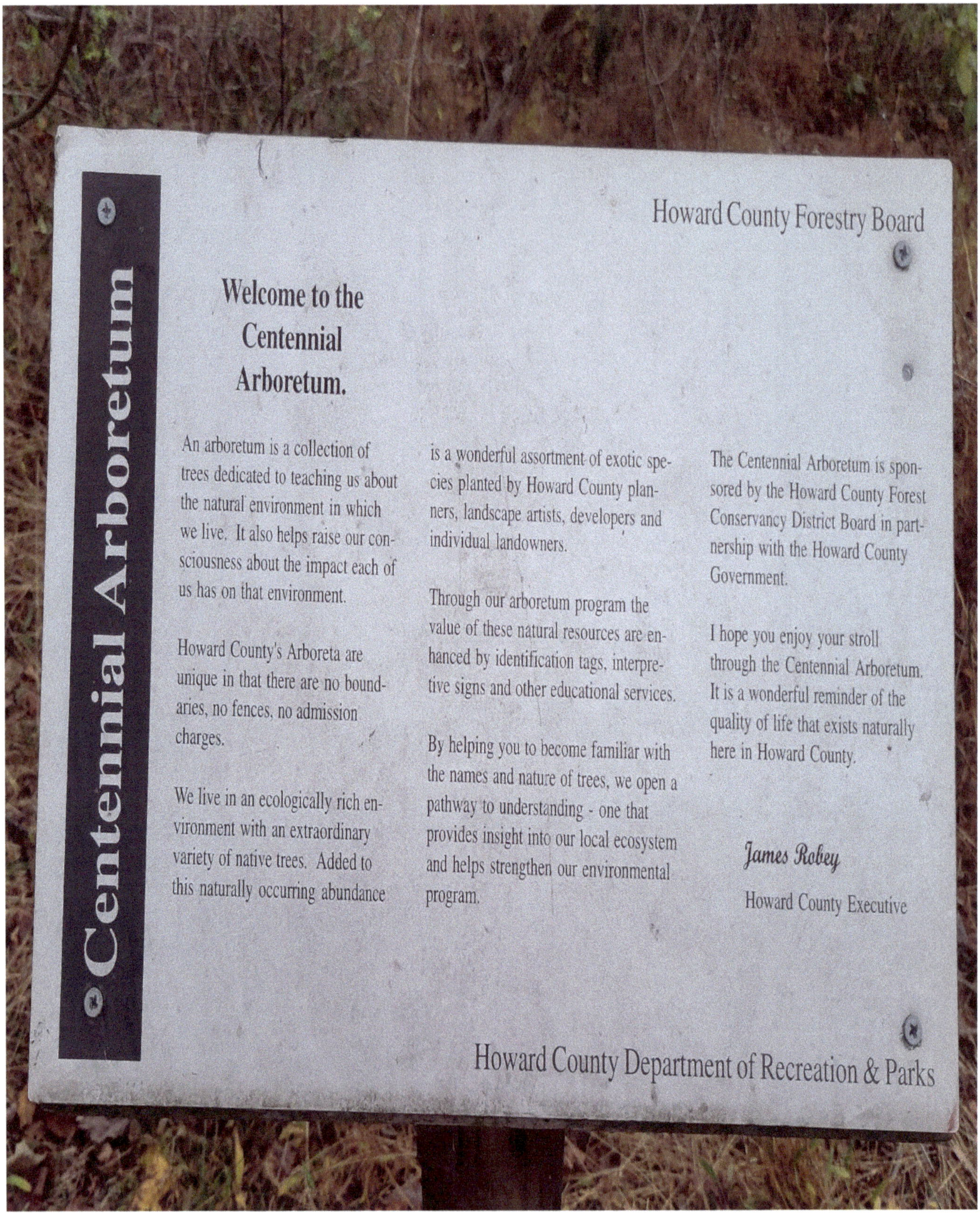

Centennial Arboretum

Howard County Forestry Board

Welcome to the Centennial Arboretum.

An arboretum is a collection of trees dedicated to teaching us about the natural environment in which we live. It also helps raise our consciousness about the impact each of us has on that environment.

Howard County's Arboreta are unique in that there are no boundaries, no fences, no admission charges.

We live in an ecologically rich environment with an extraordinary variety of native trees. Added to this naturally occurring abundance is a wonderful assortment of exotic species planted by Howard County planners, landscape artists, developers and individual landowners.

Through our arboretum program the value of these natural resources are enhanced by identification tags, interpretive signs and other educational services.

By helping you to become familiar with the names and nature of trees, we open a pathway to understanding - one that provides insight into our local ecosystem and helps strengthen our environmental program.

The Centennial Arboretum is sponsored by the Howard County Forest Conservancy District Board in partnership with the Howard County Government.

I hope you enjoy your stroll through the Centennial Arboretum. It is a wonderful reminder of the quality of life that exists naturally here in Howard County.

James Robey
Howard County Executive

Howard County Department of Recreation & Parks

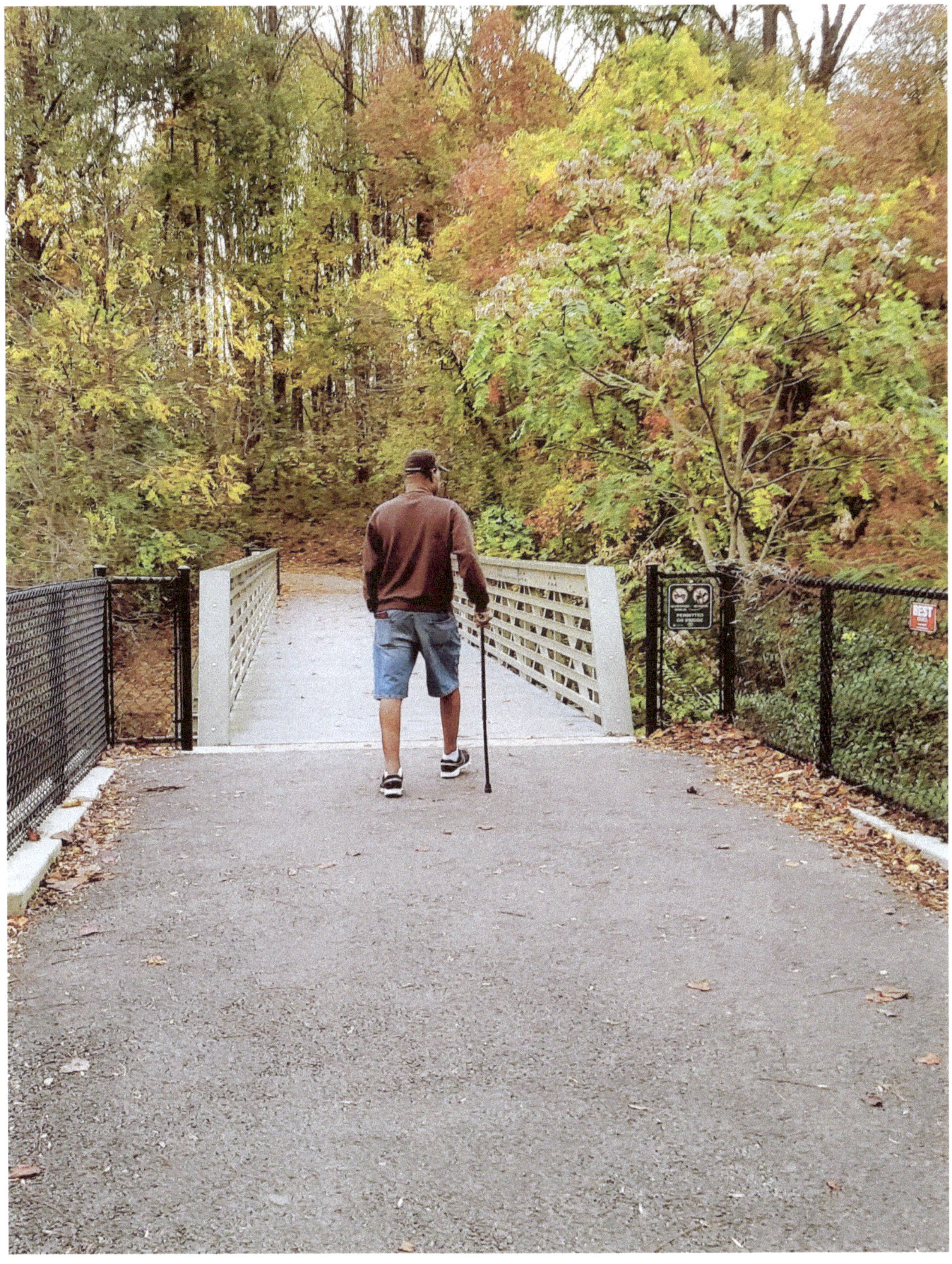

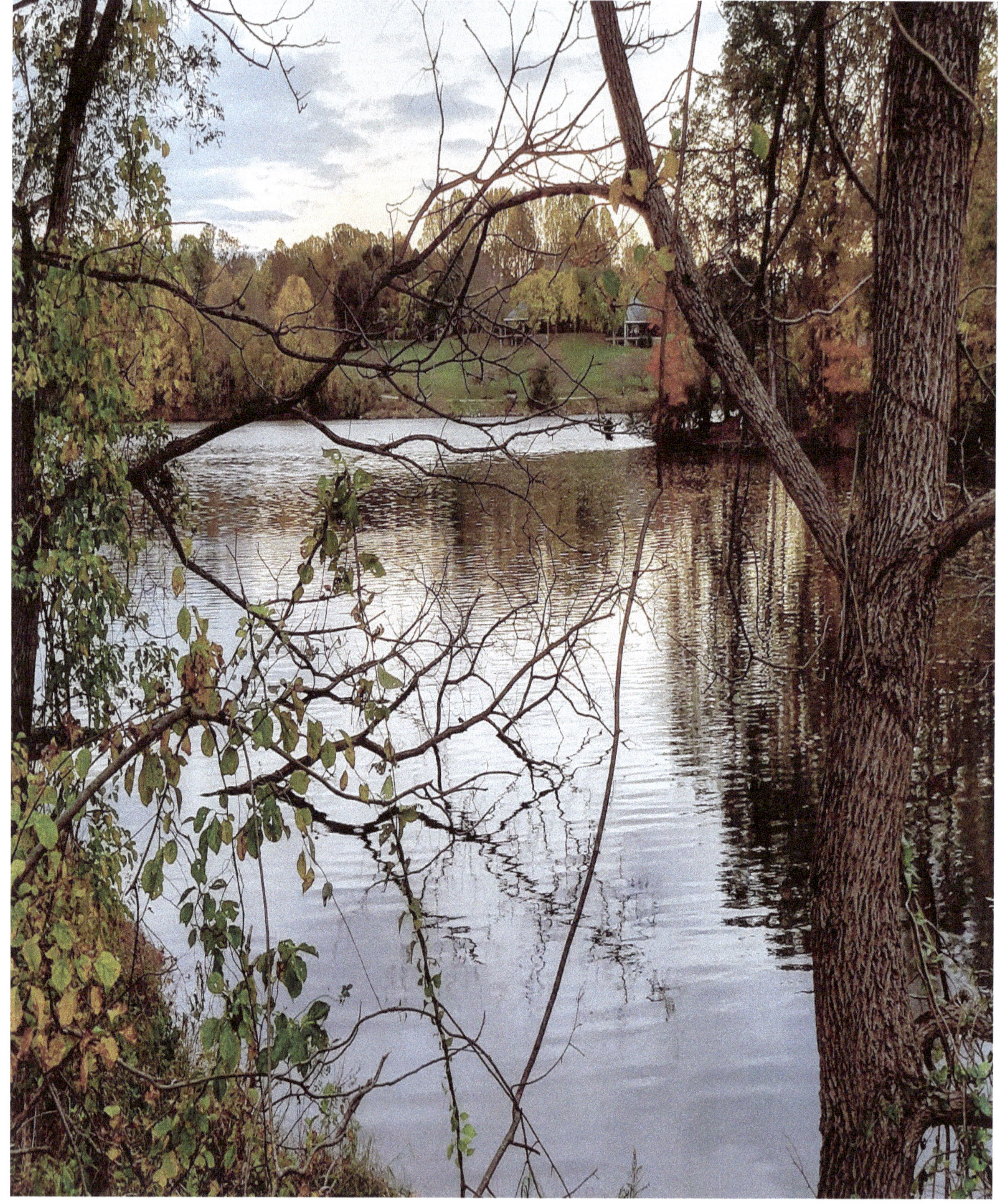

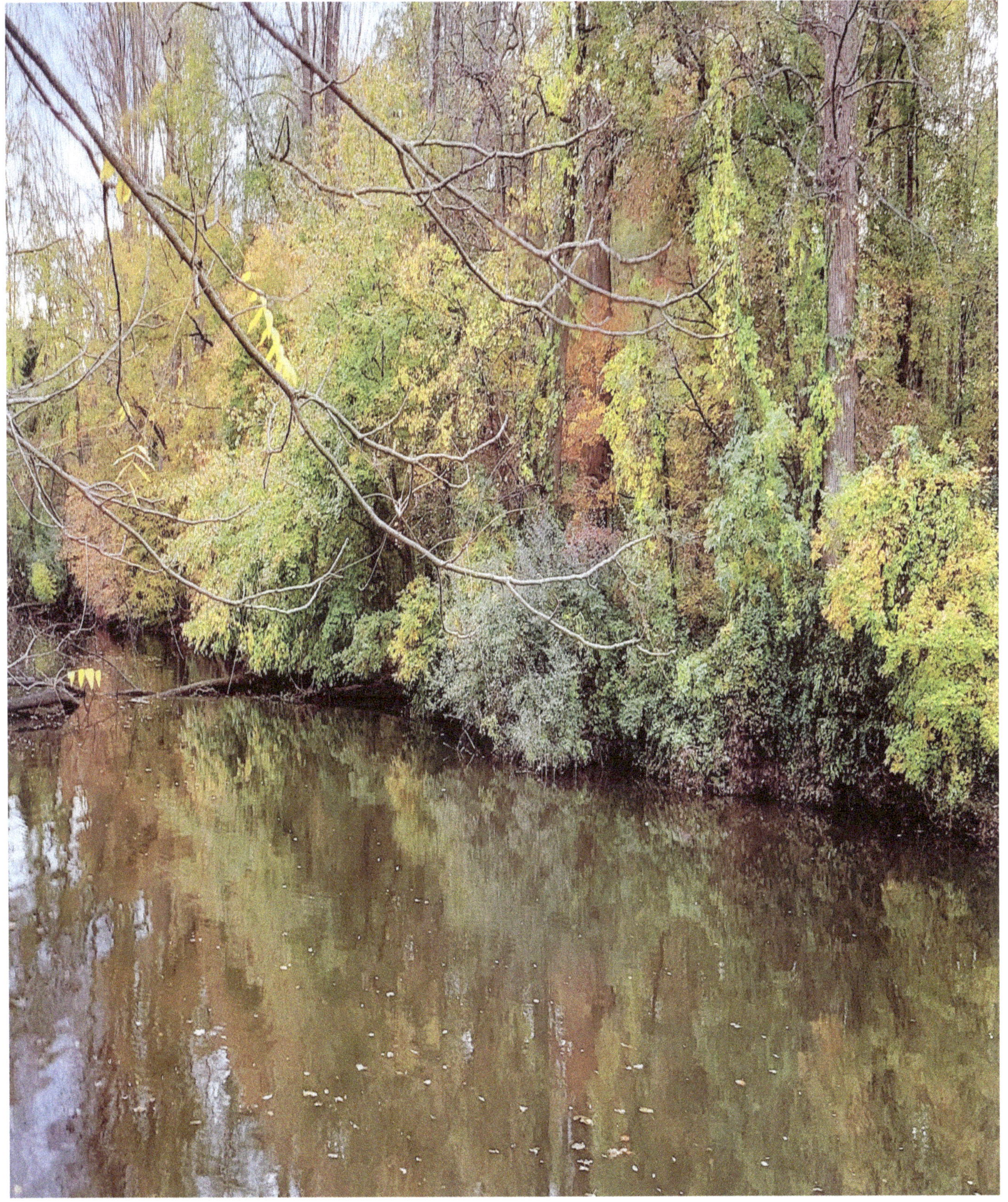

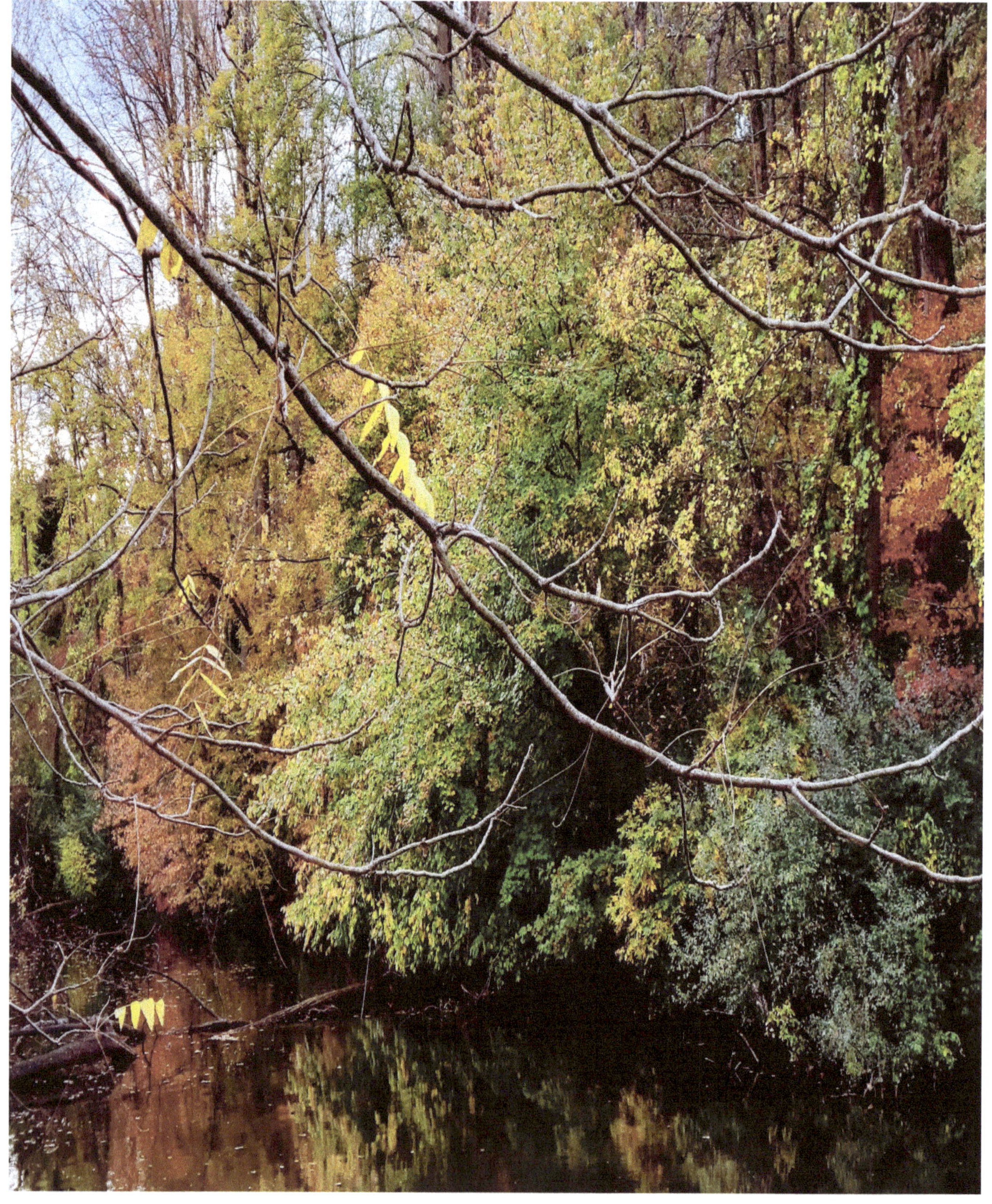

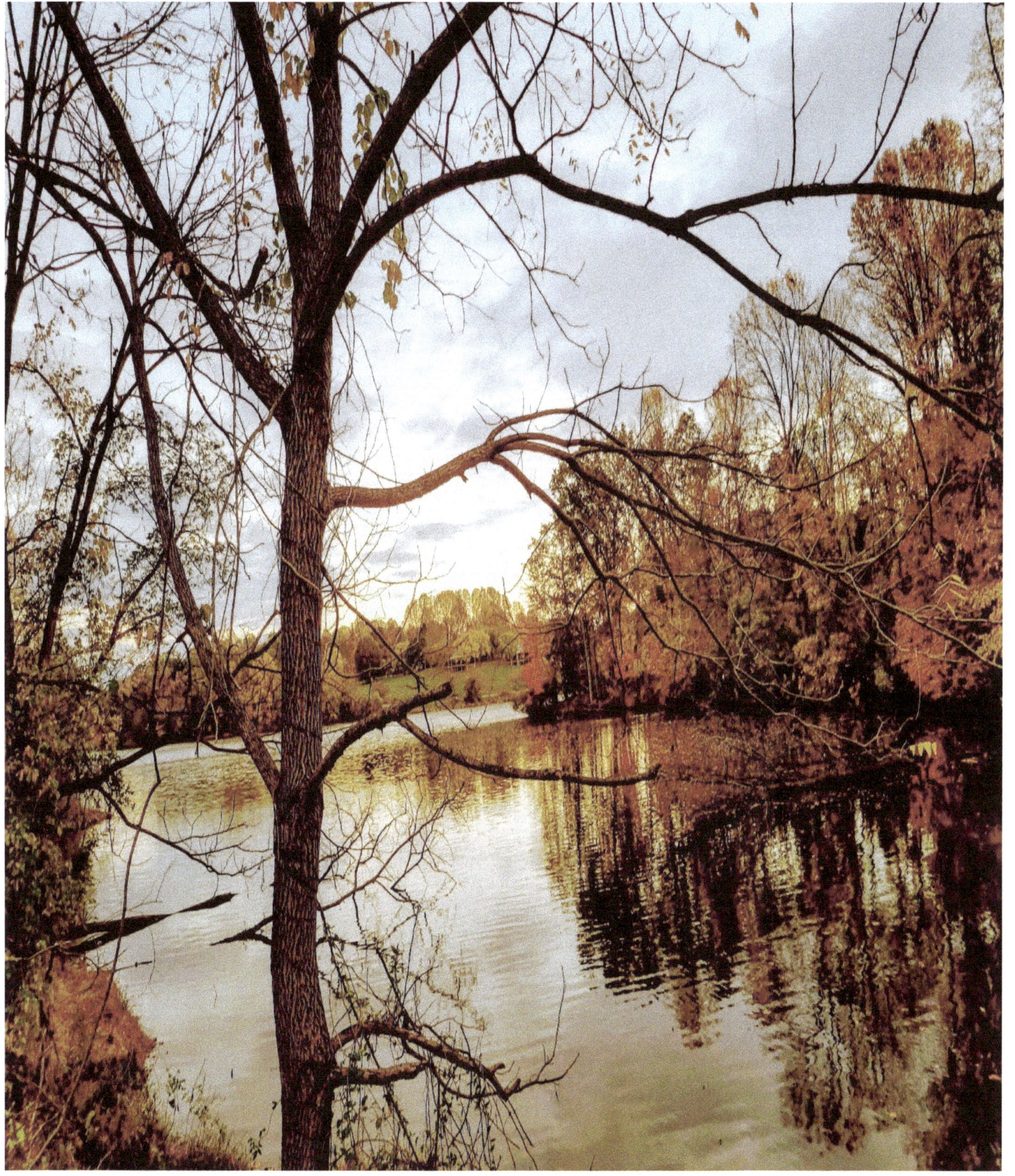

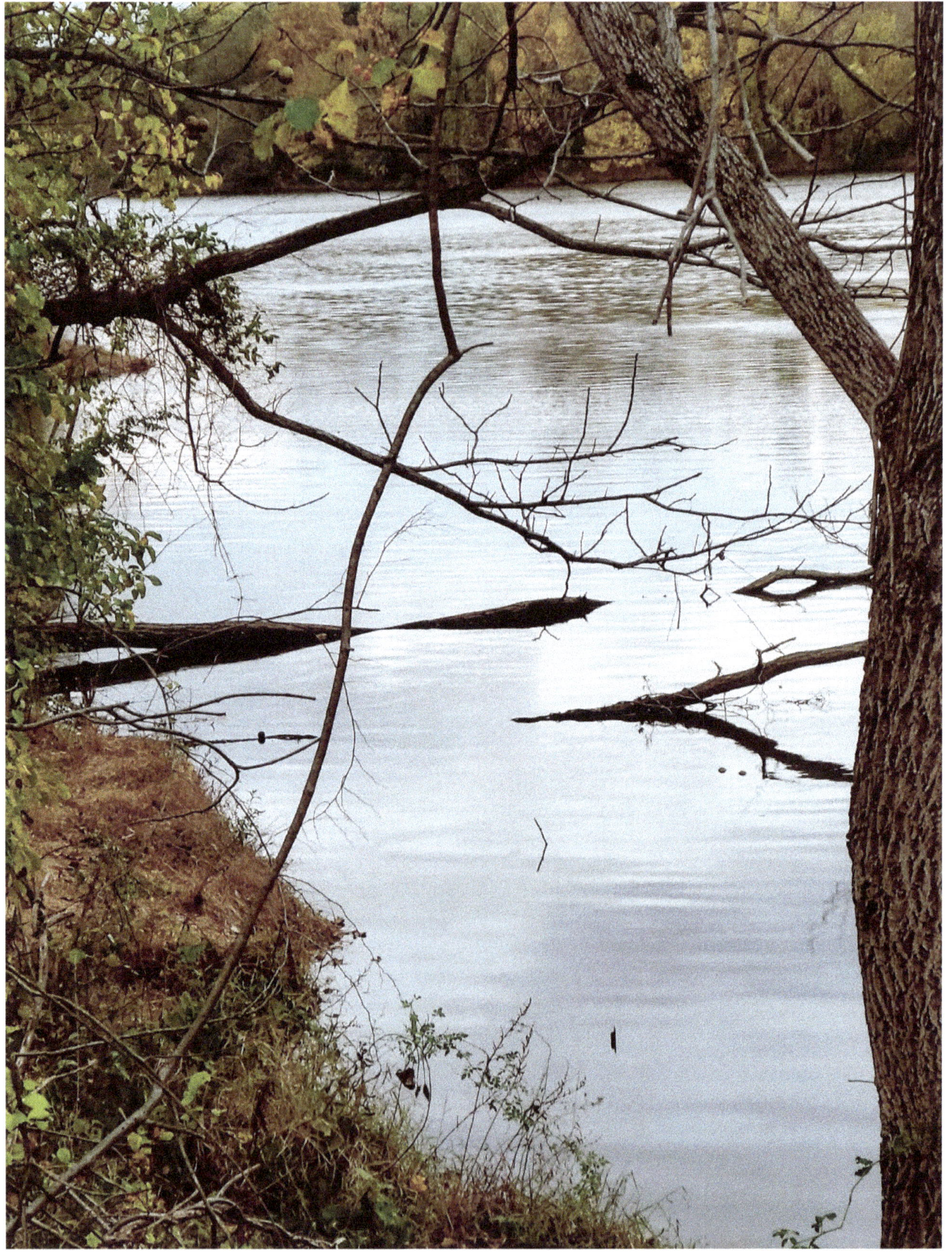

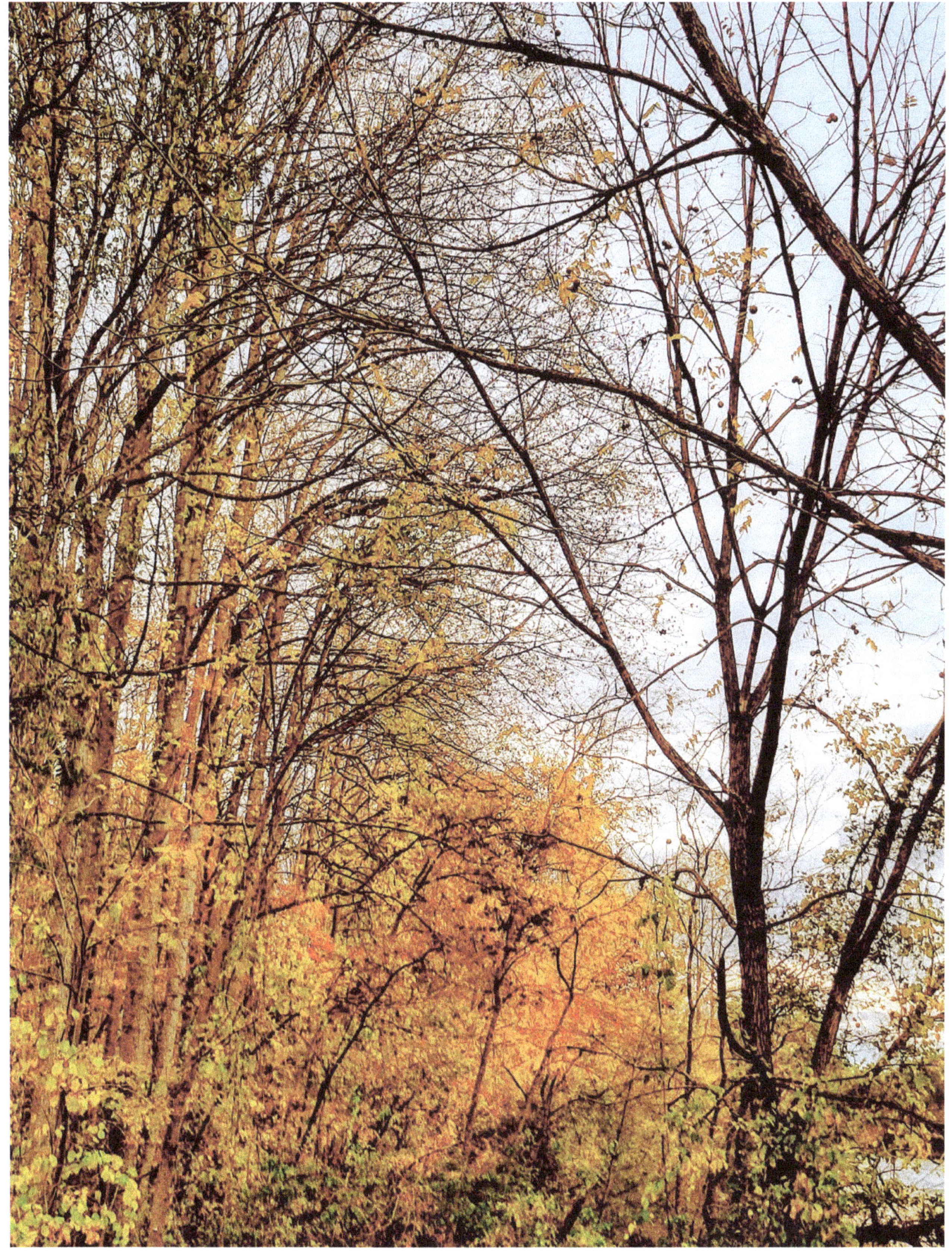

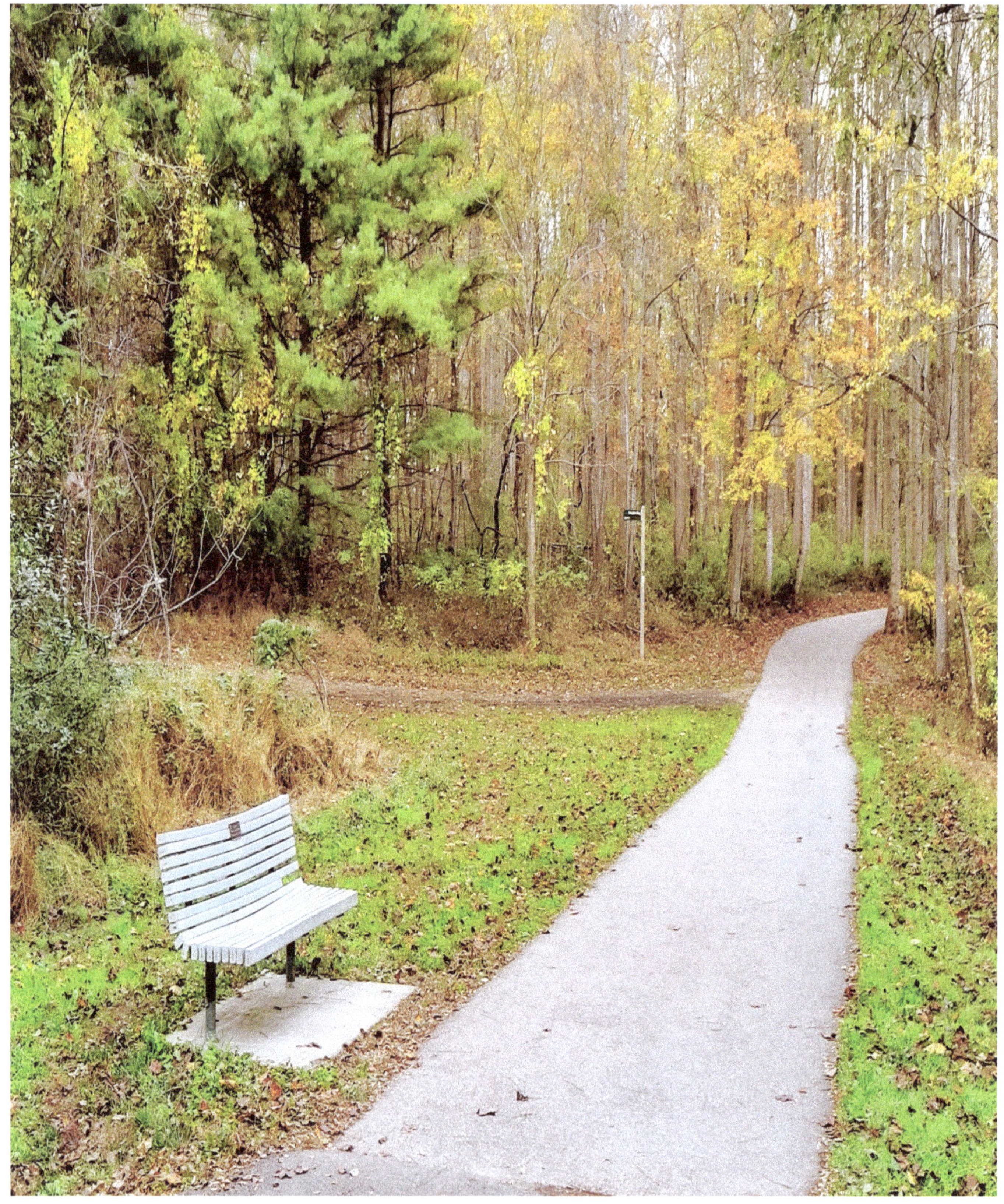

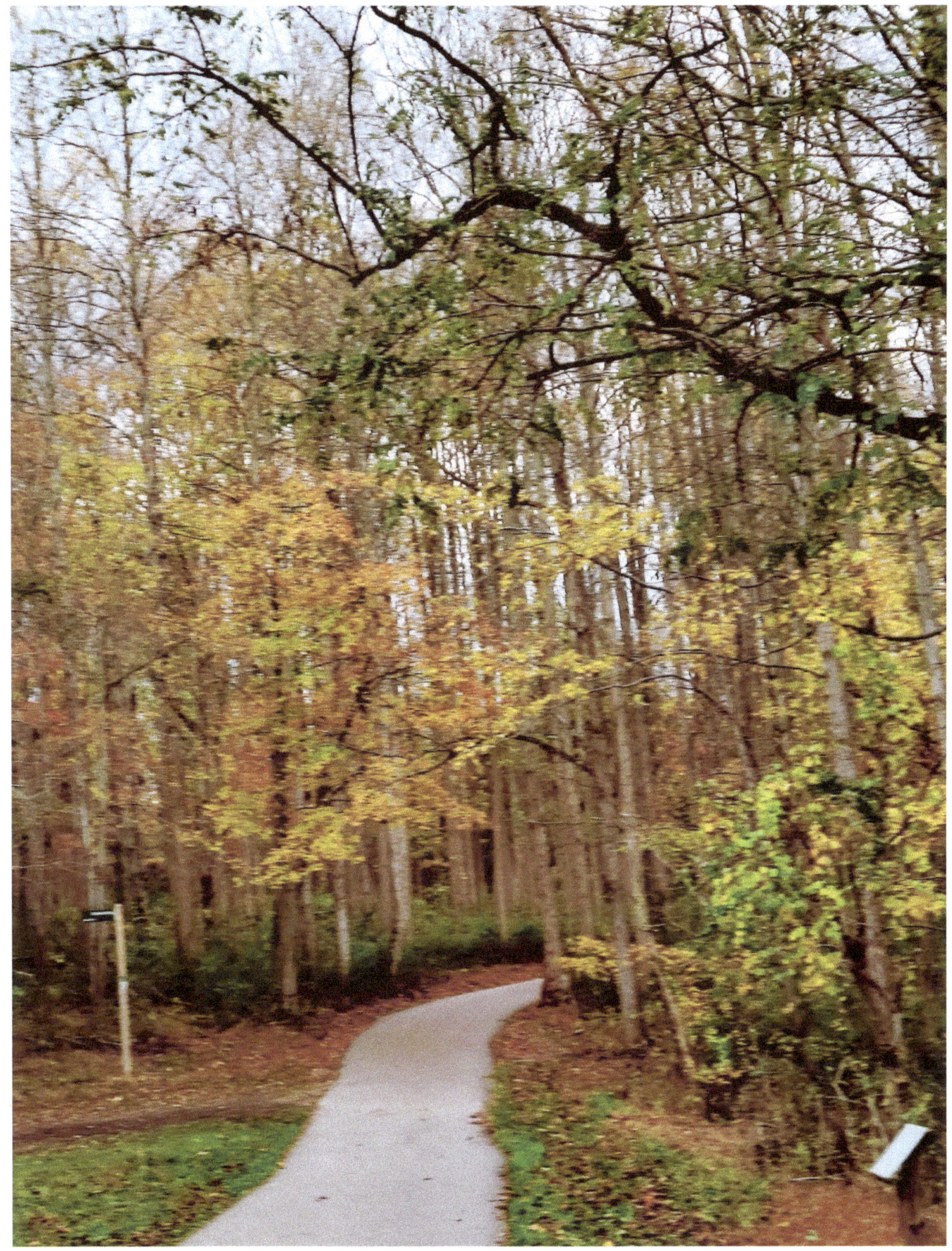

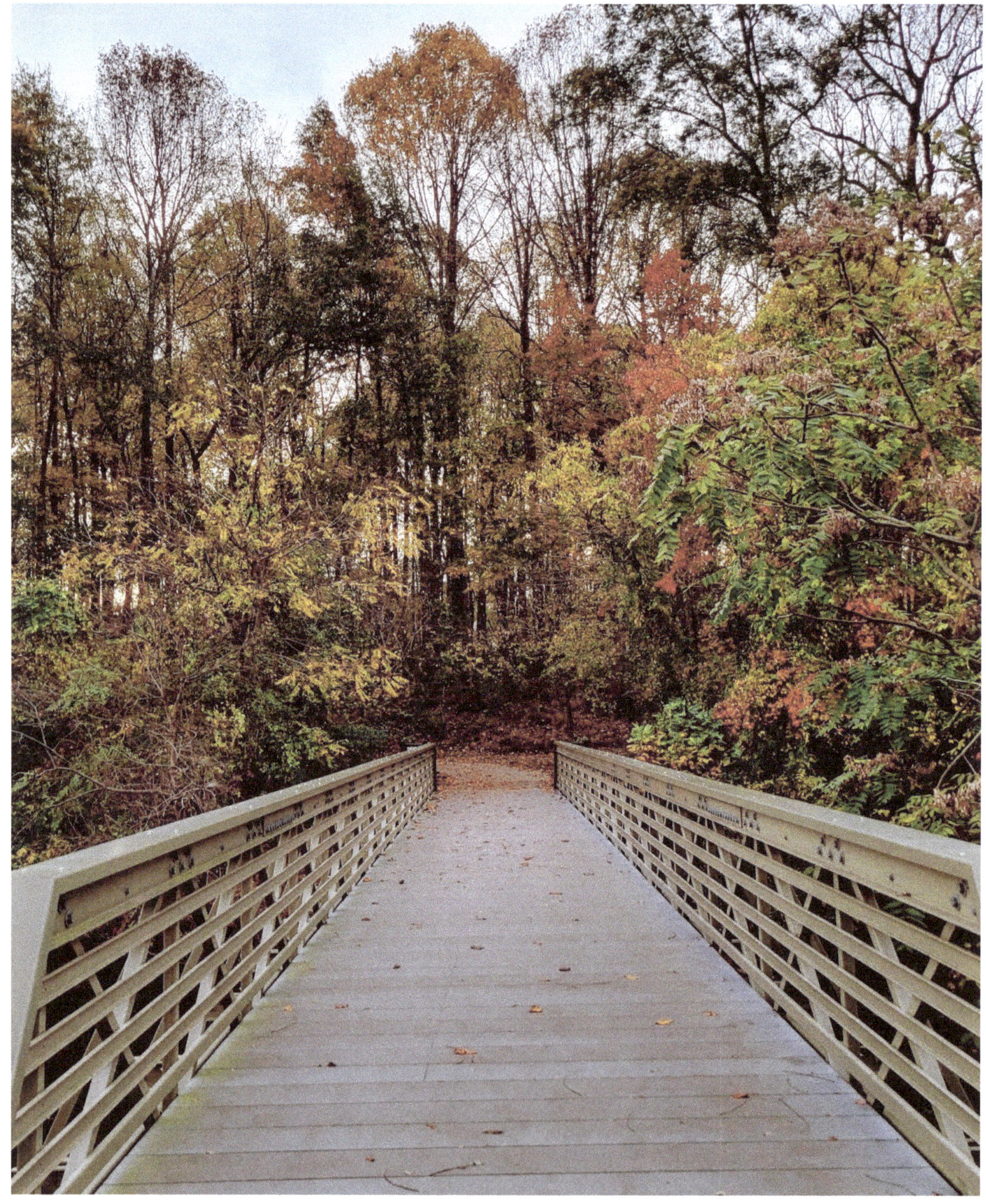

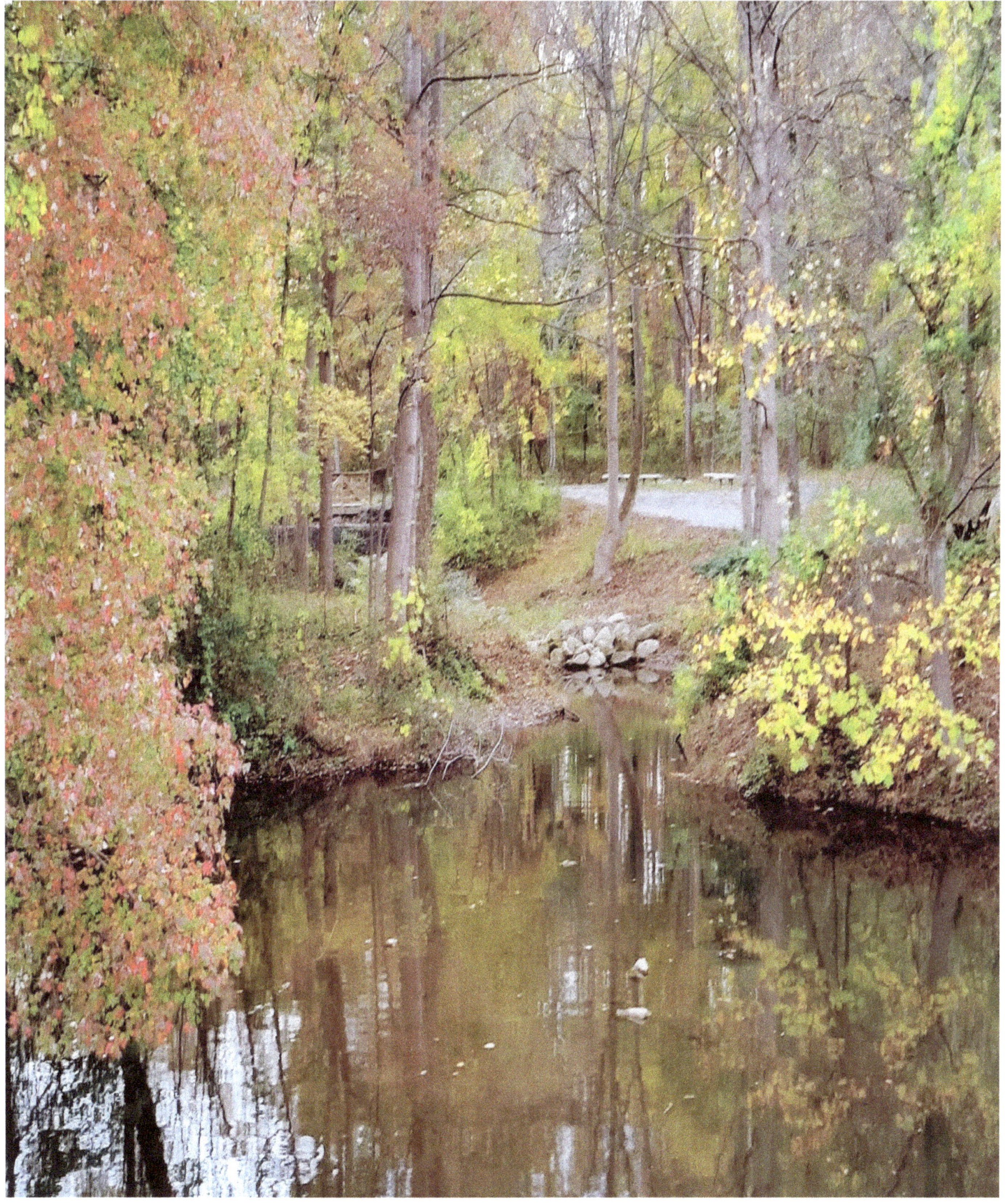

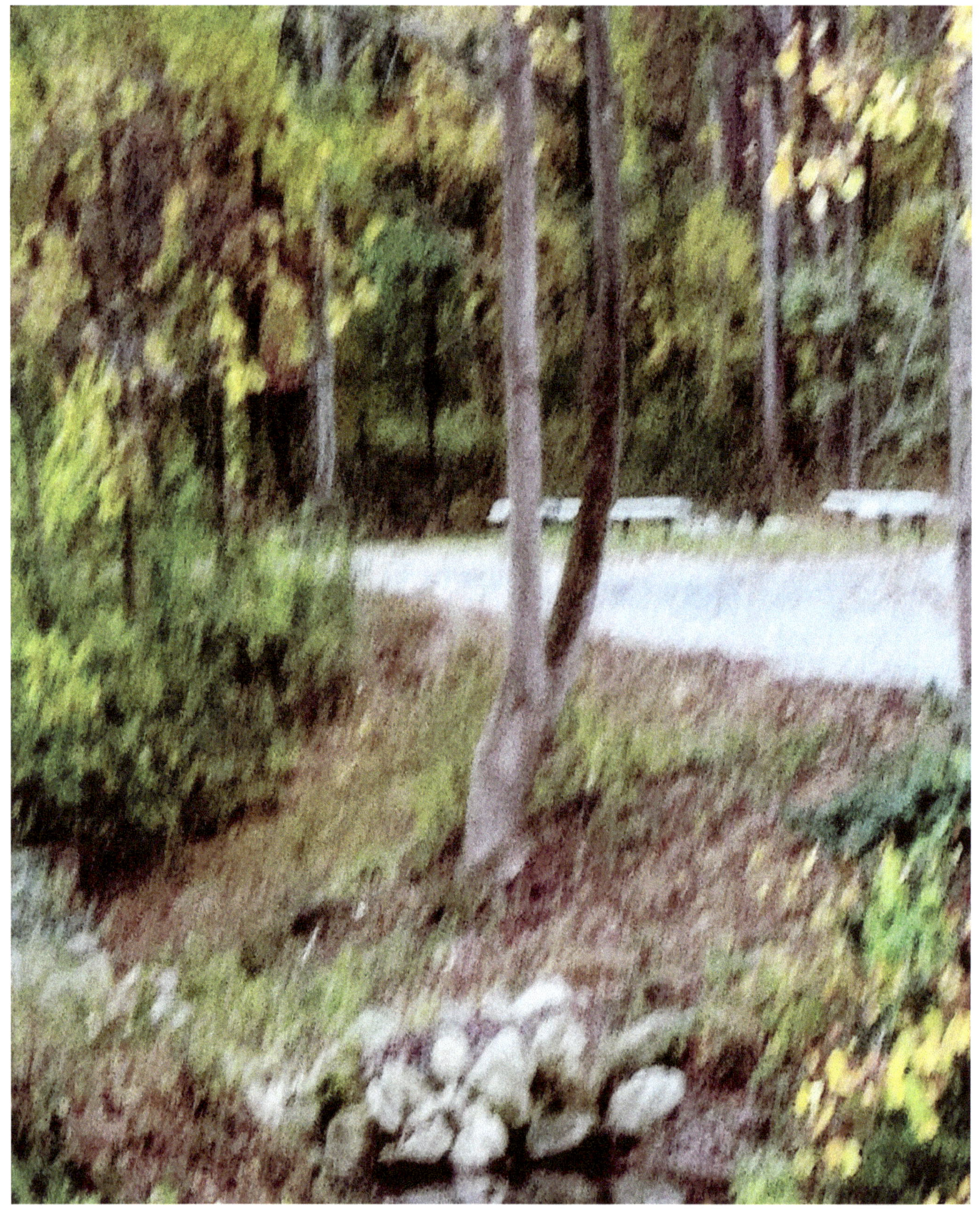

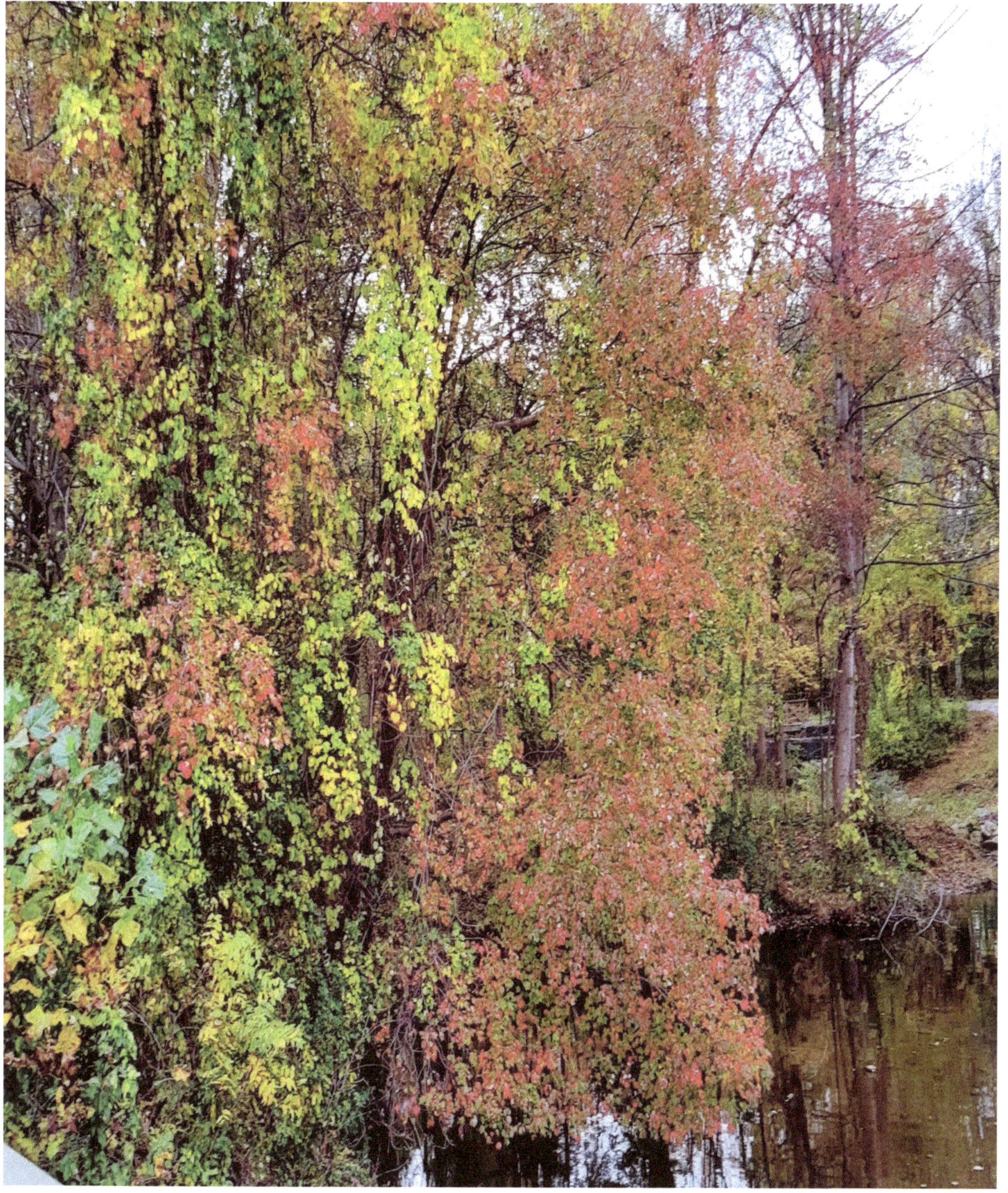

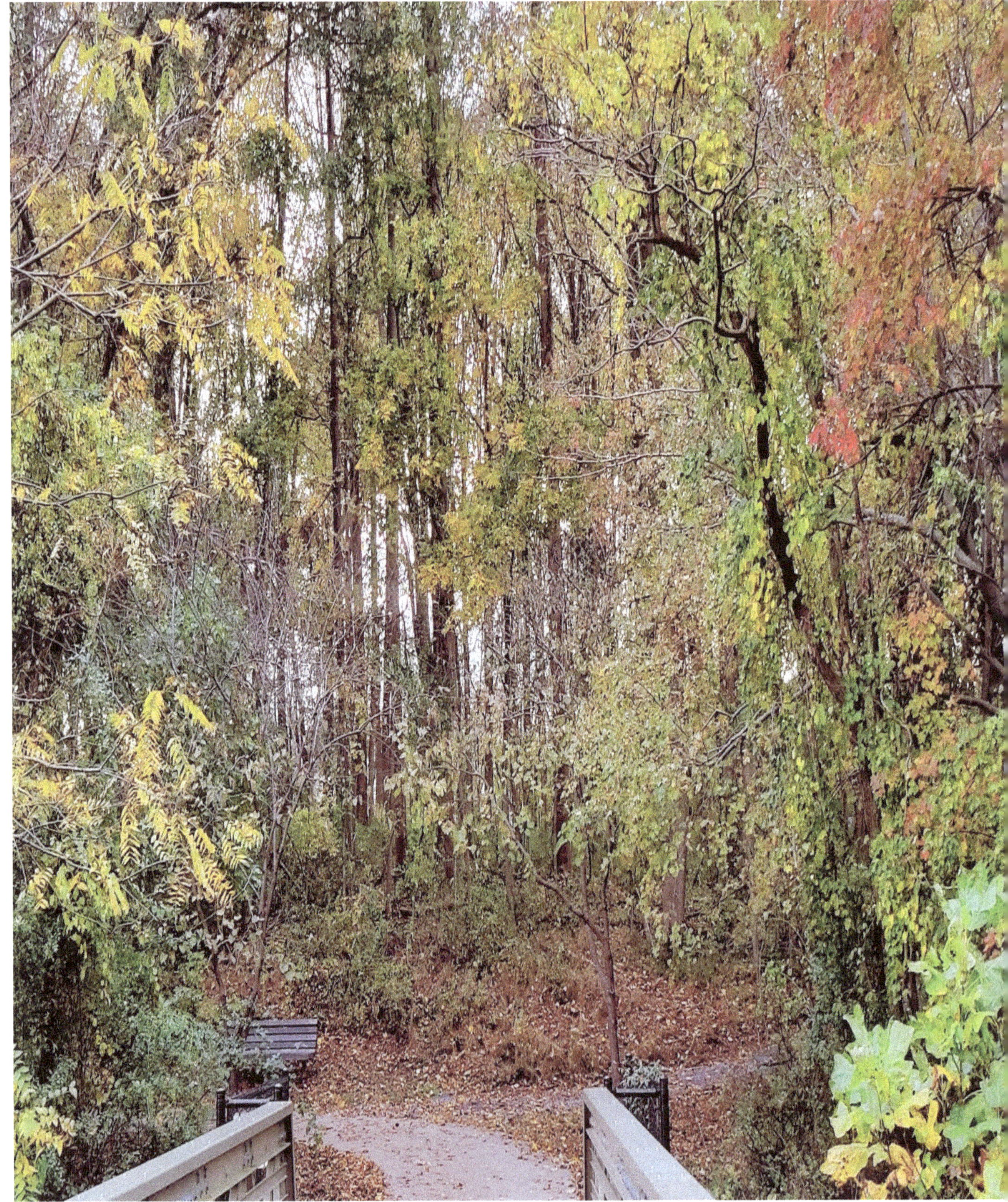

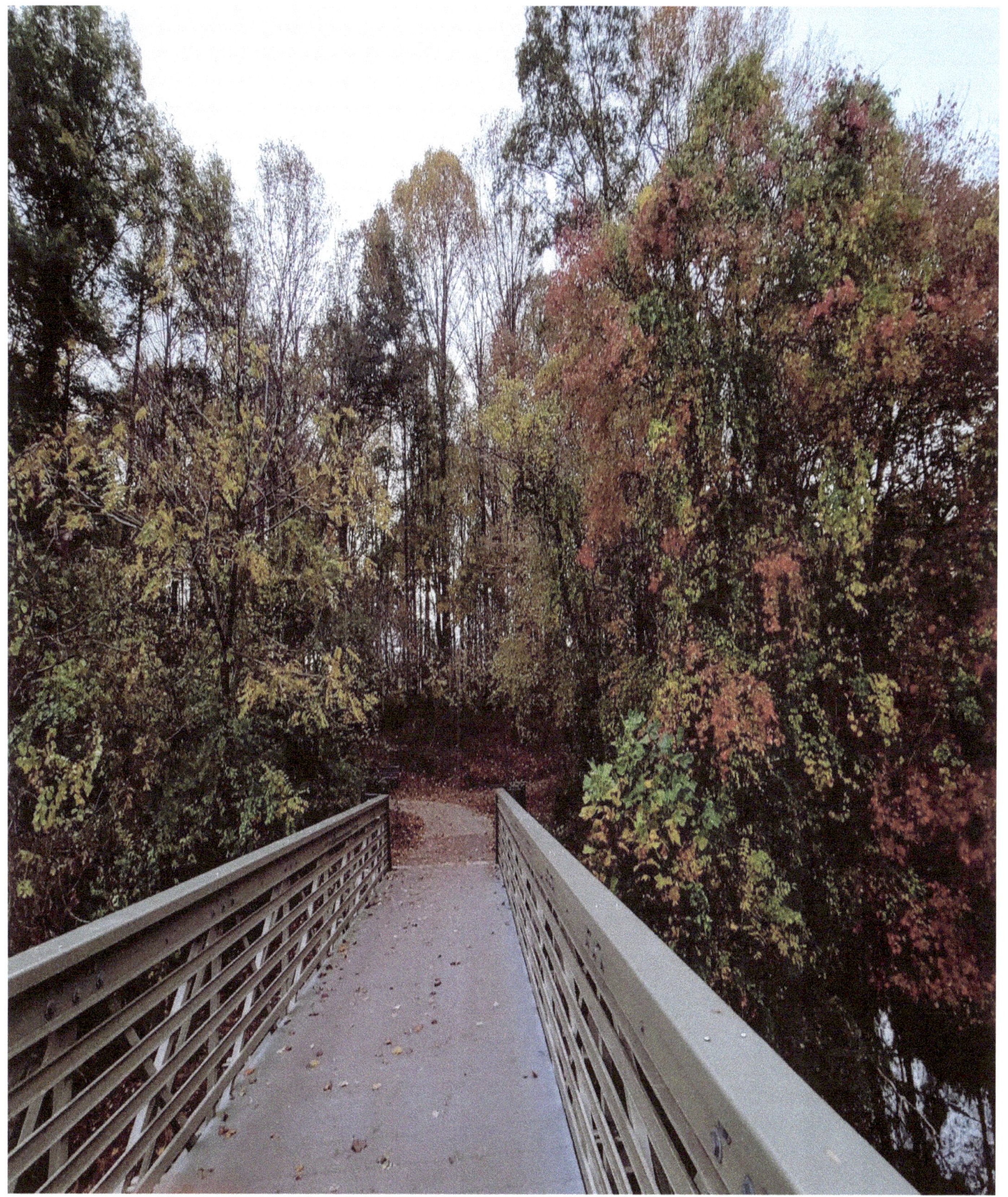

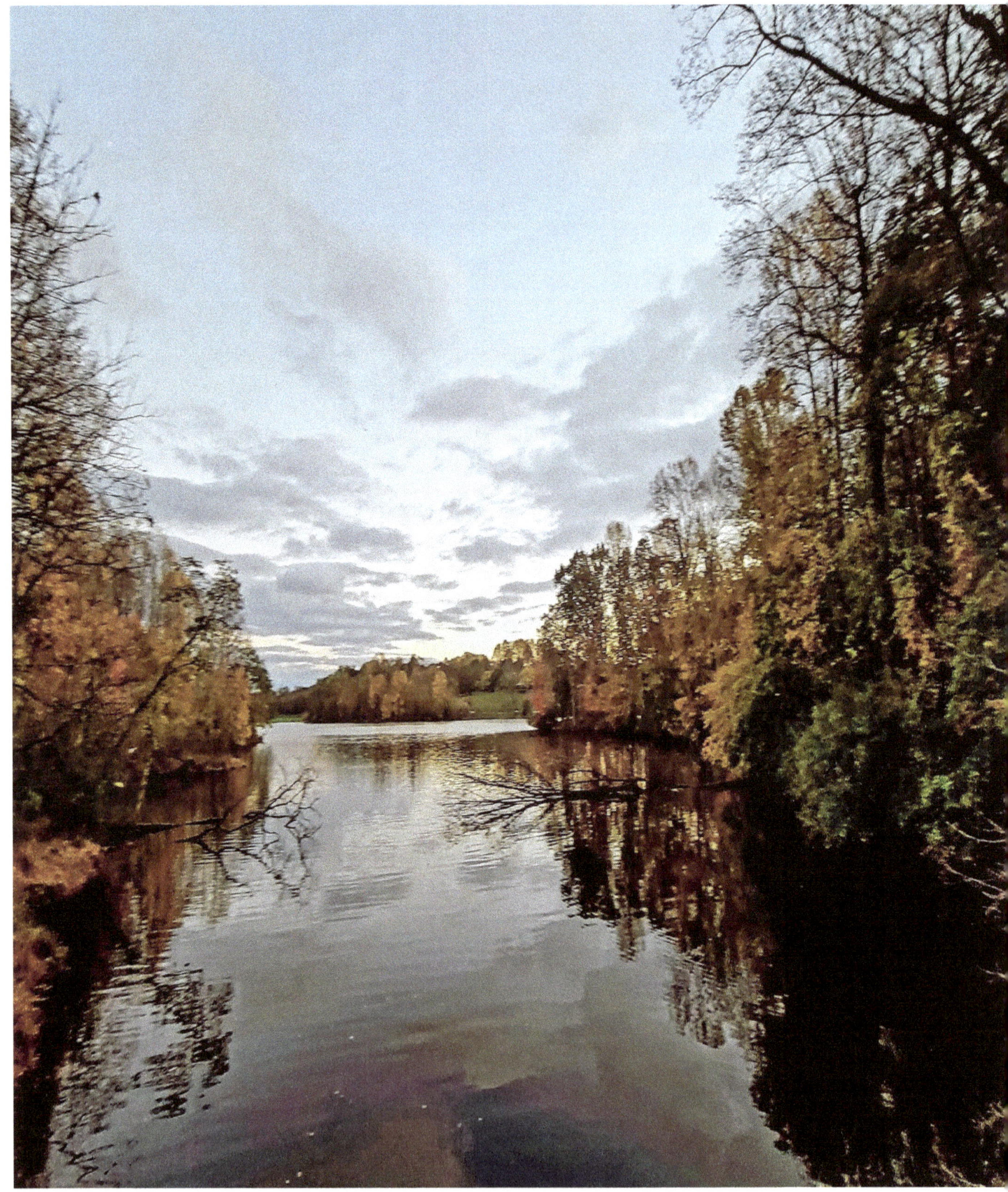

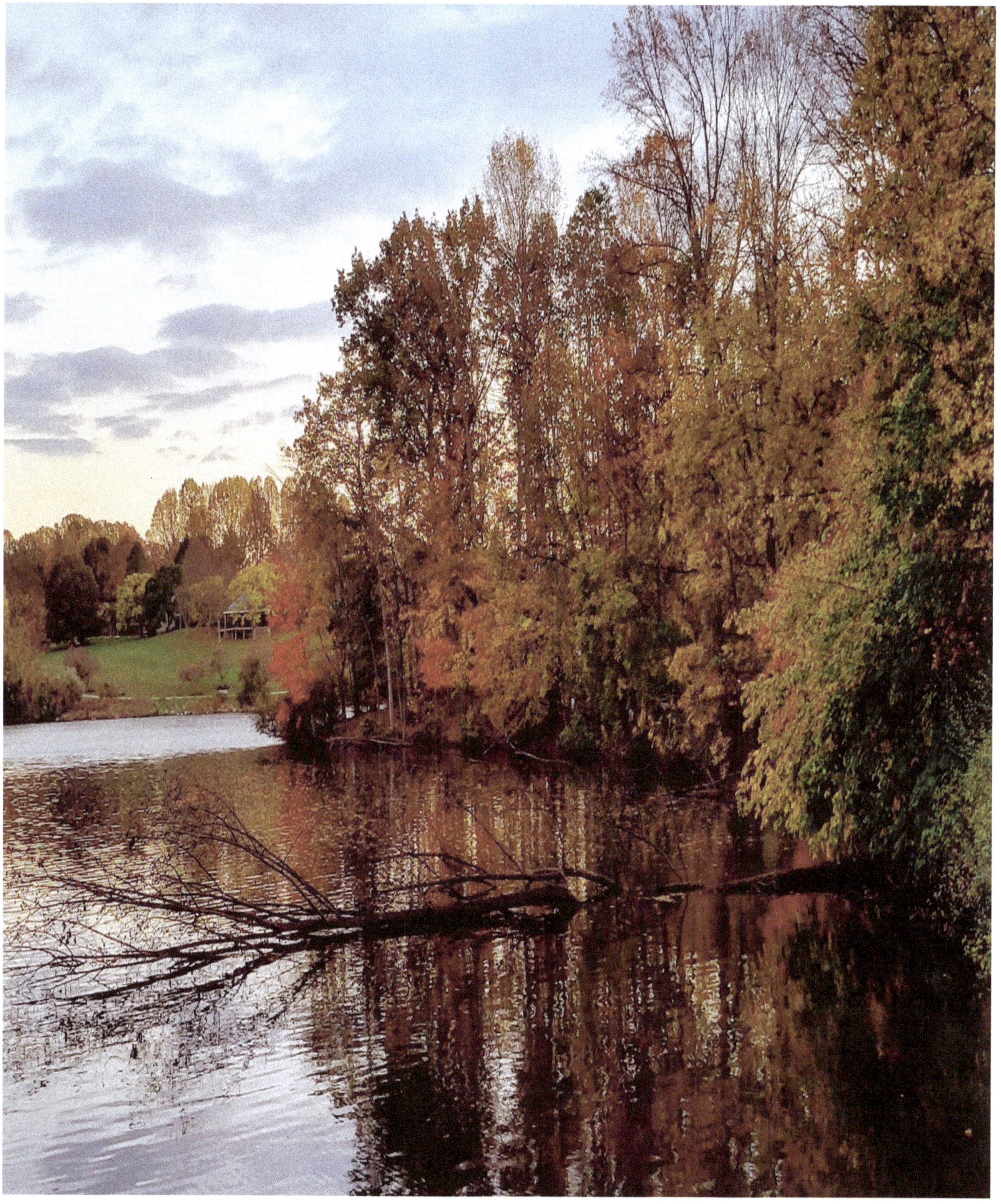

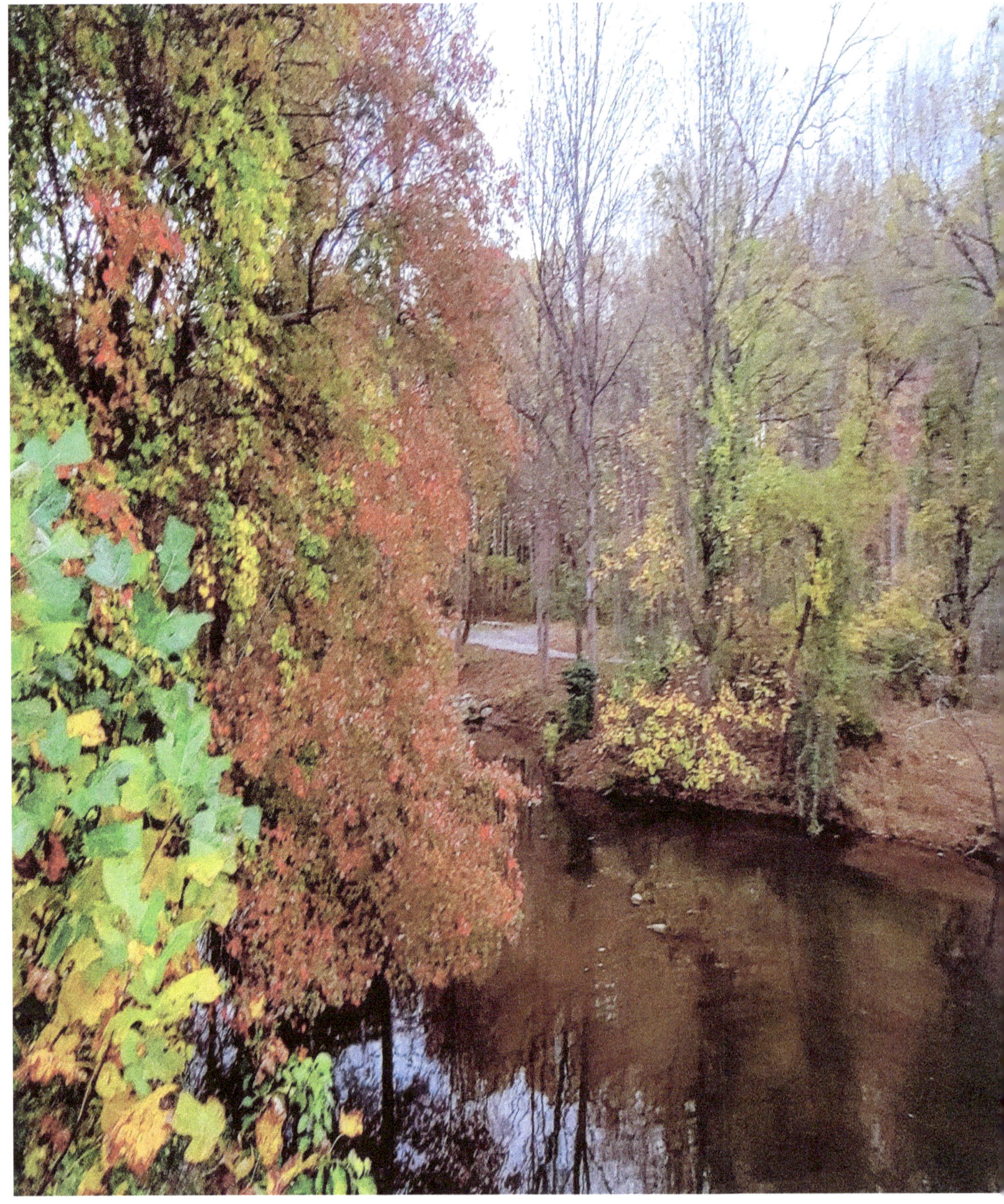

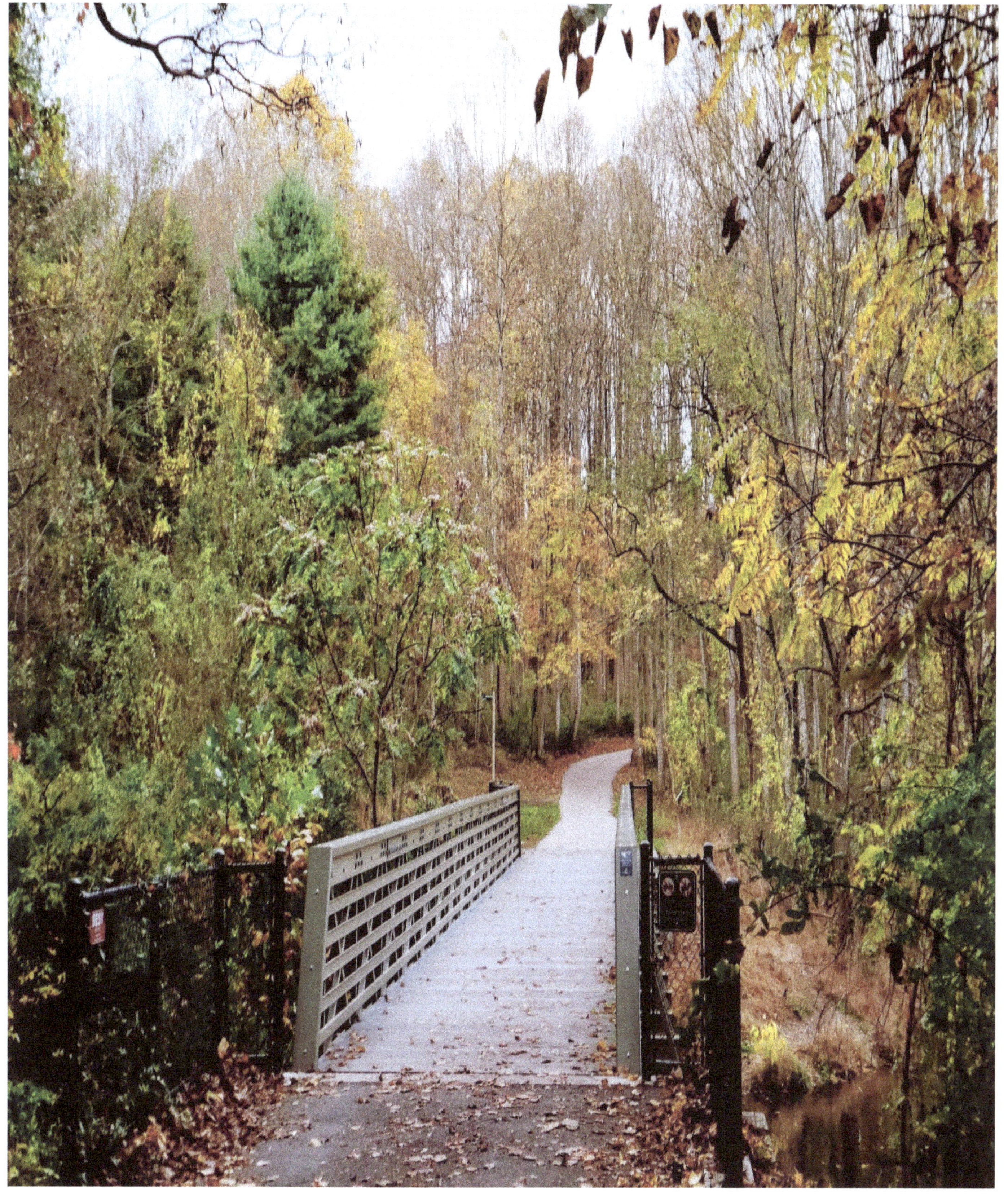

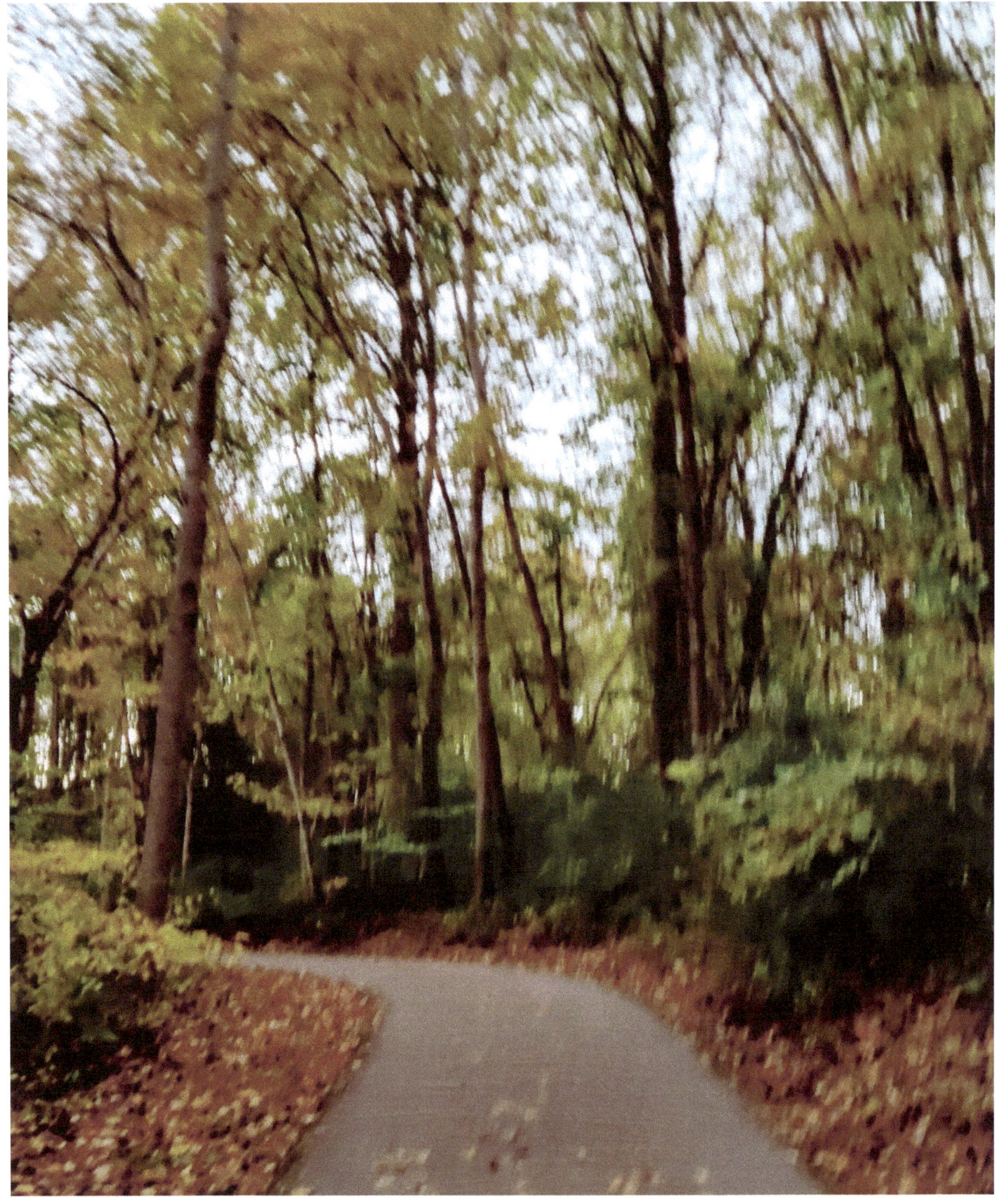

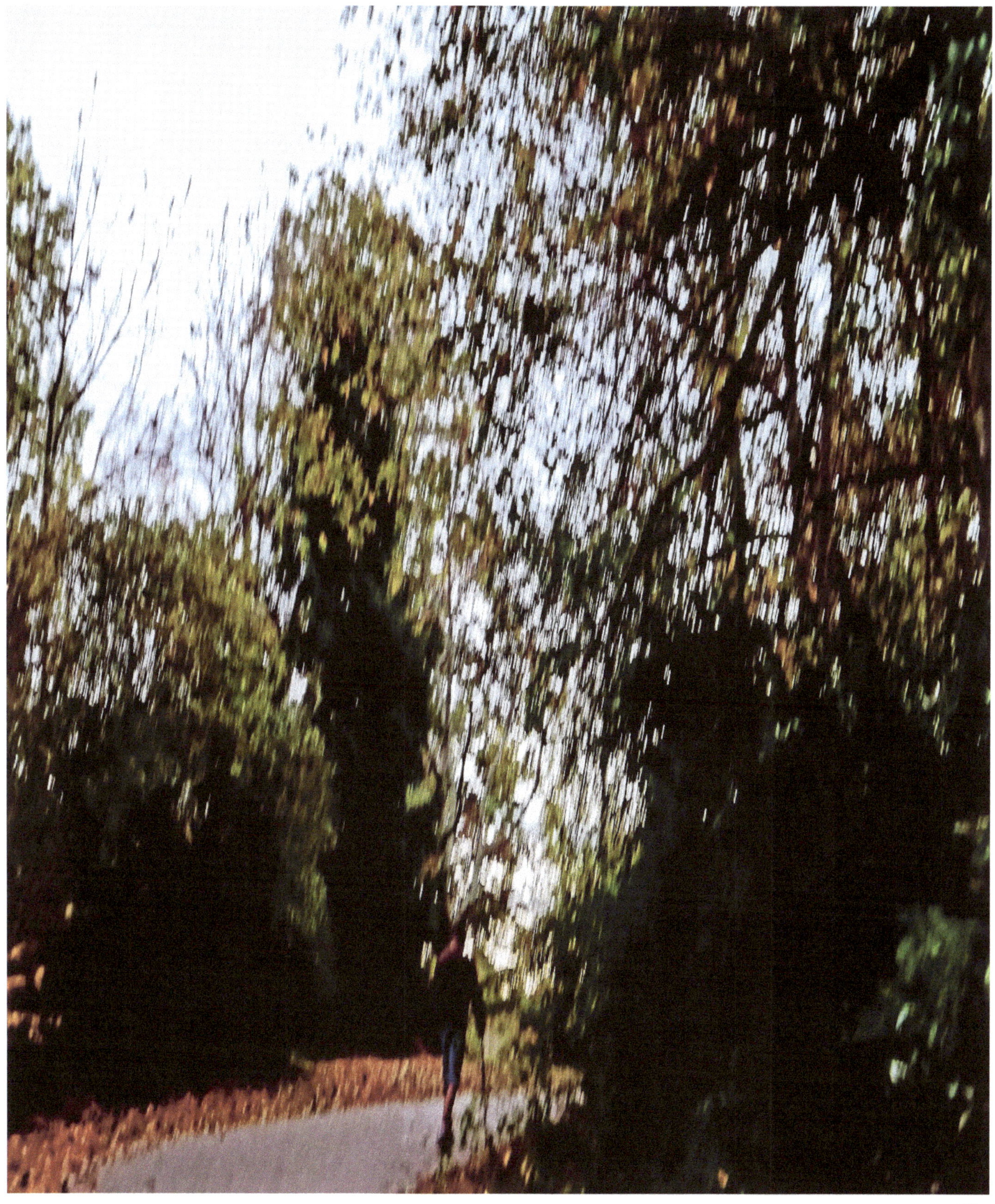

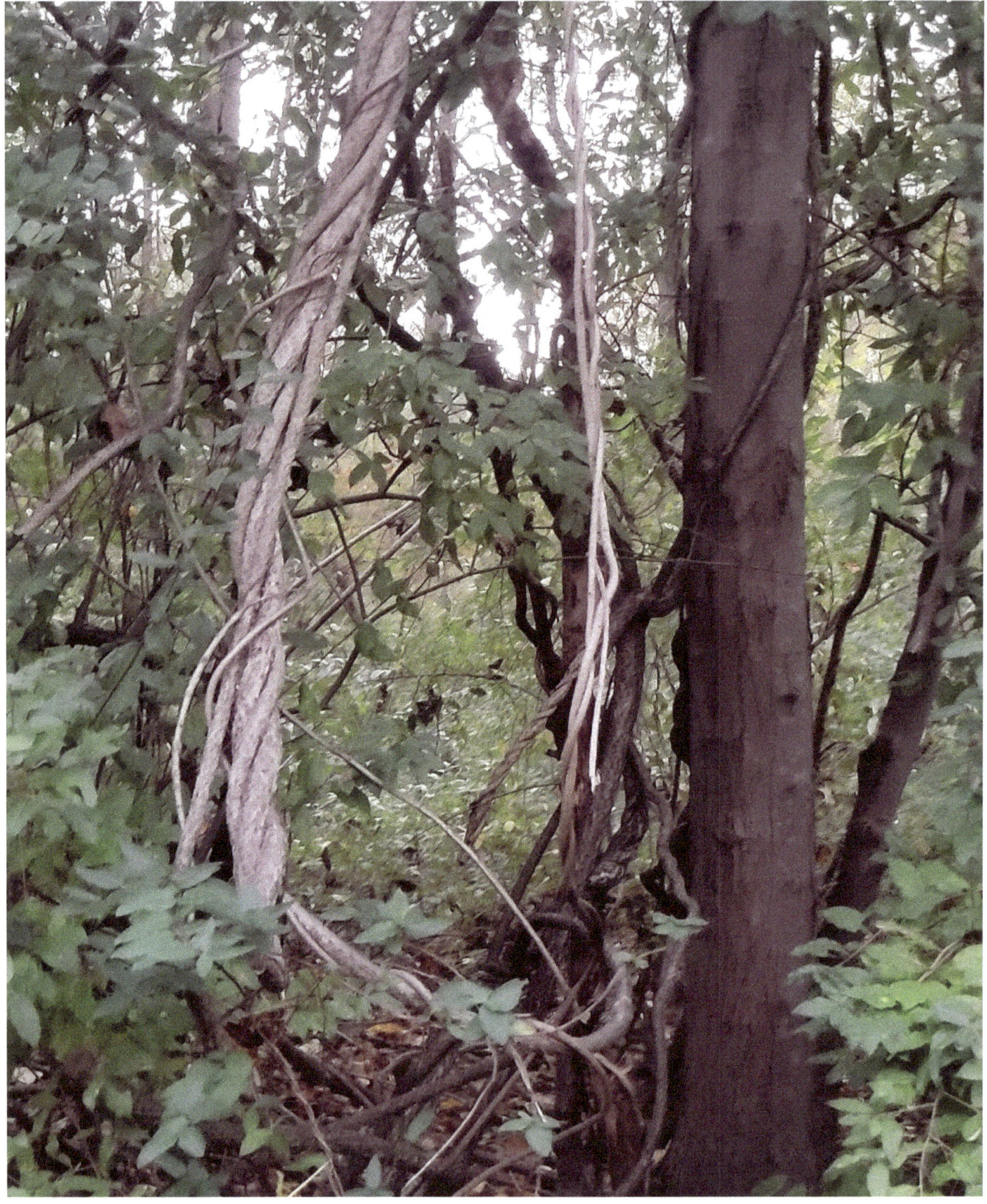

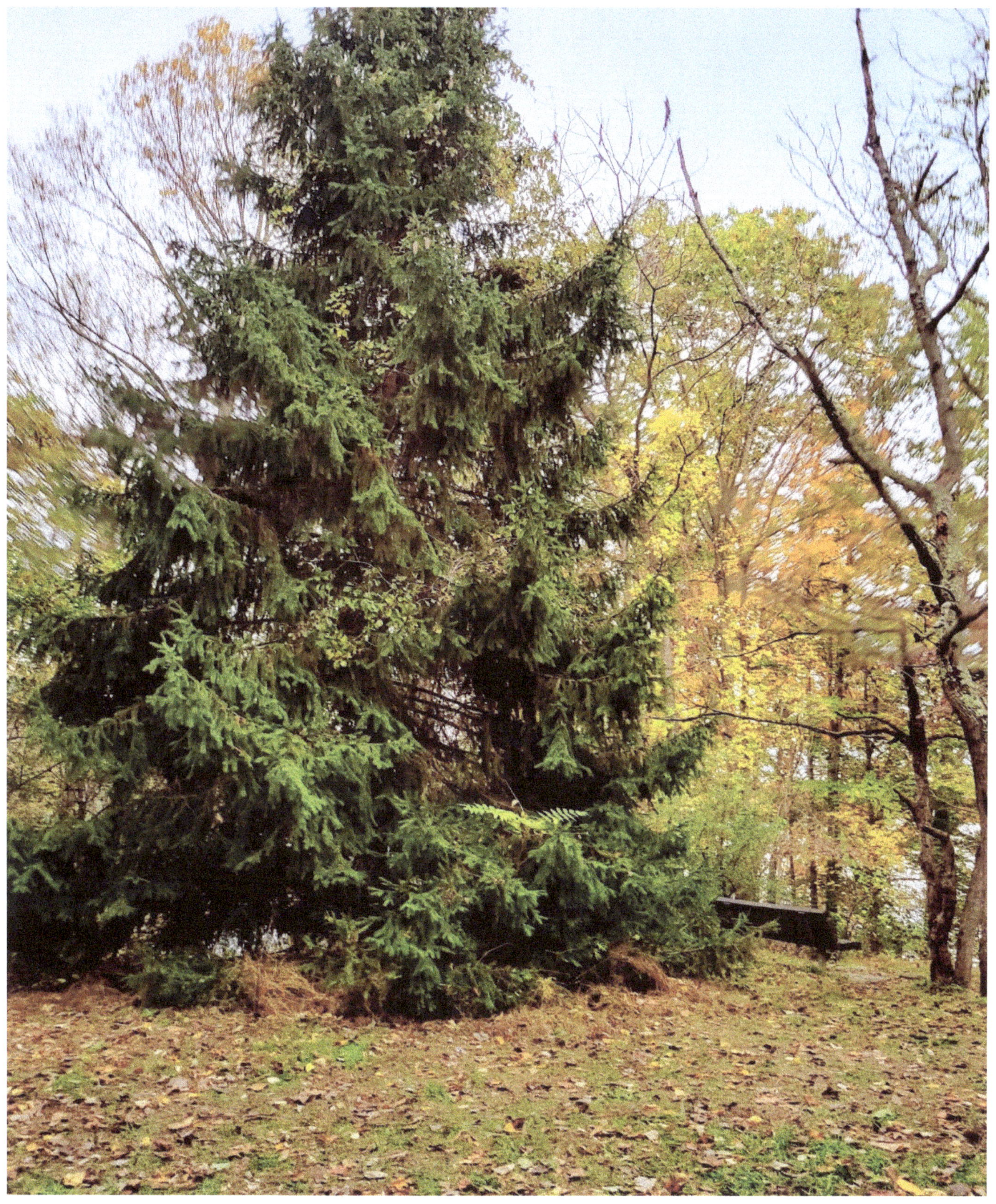

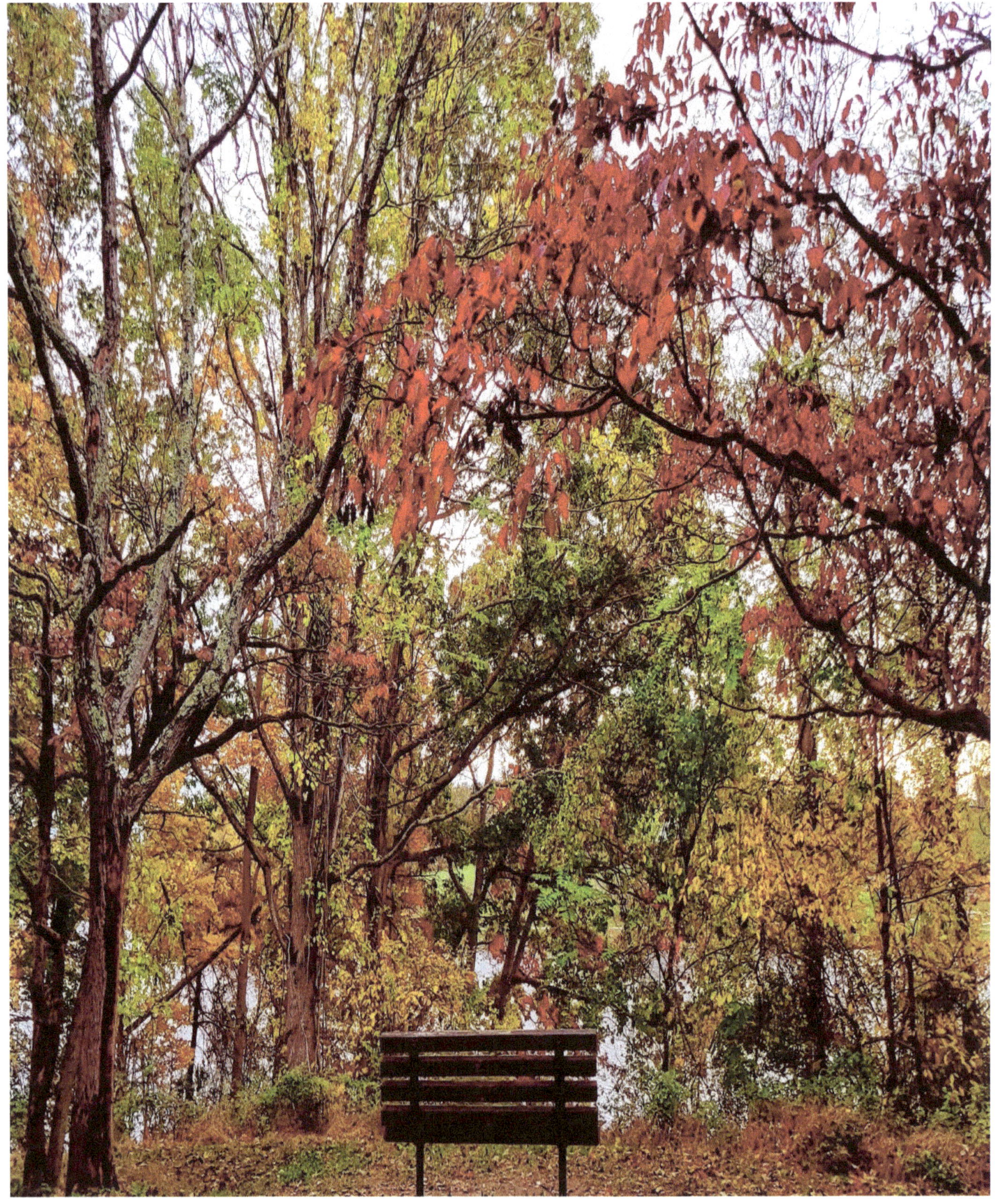

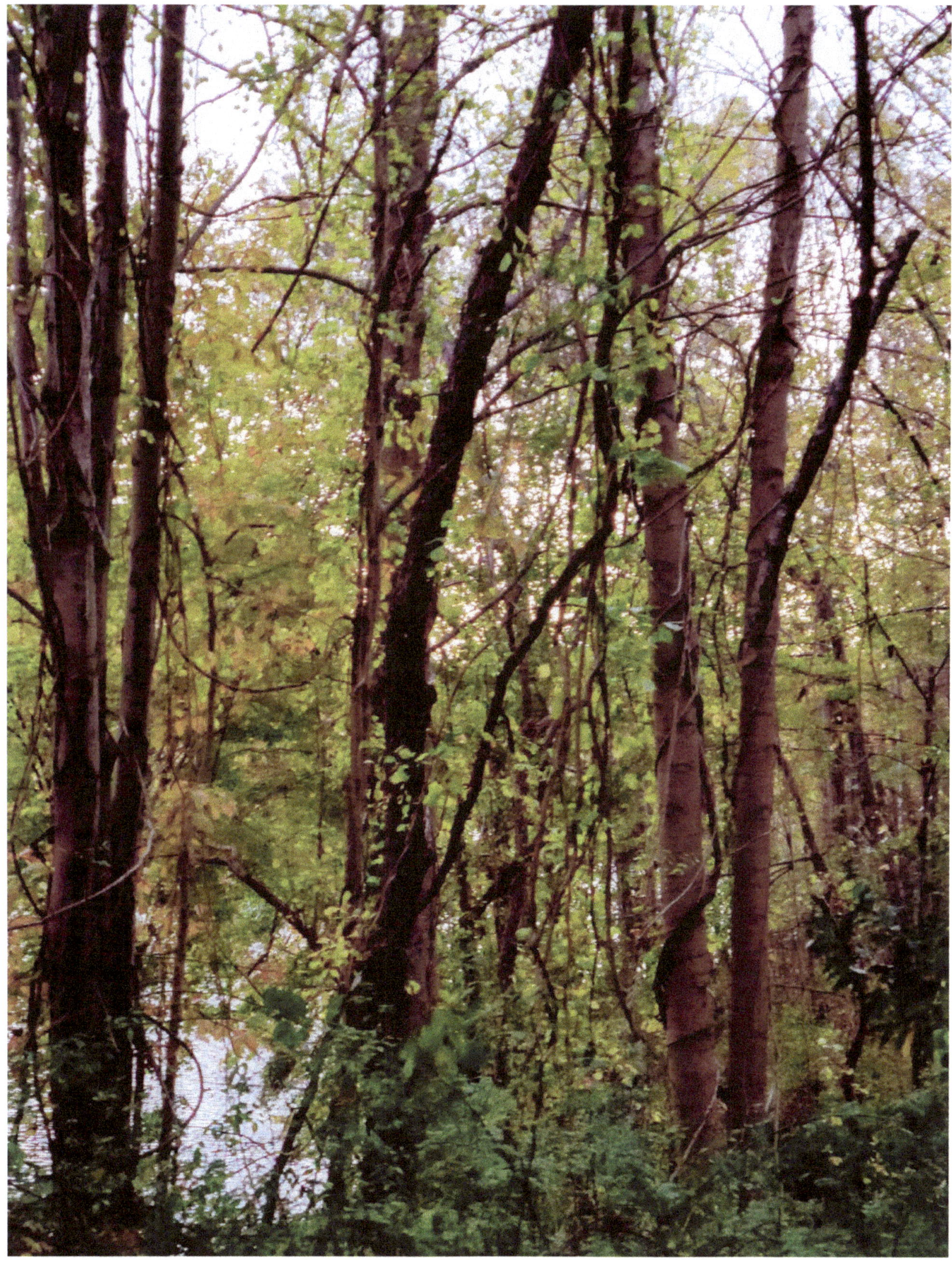

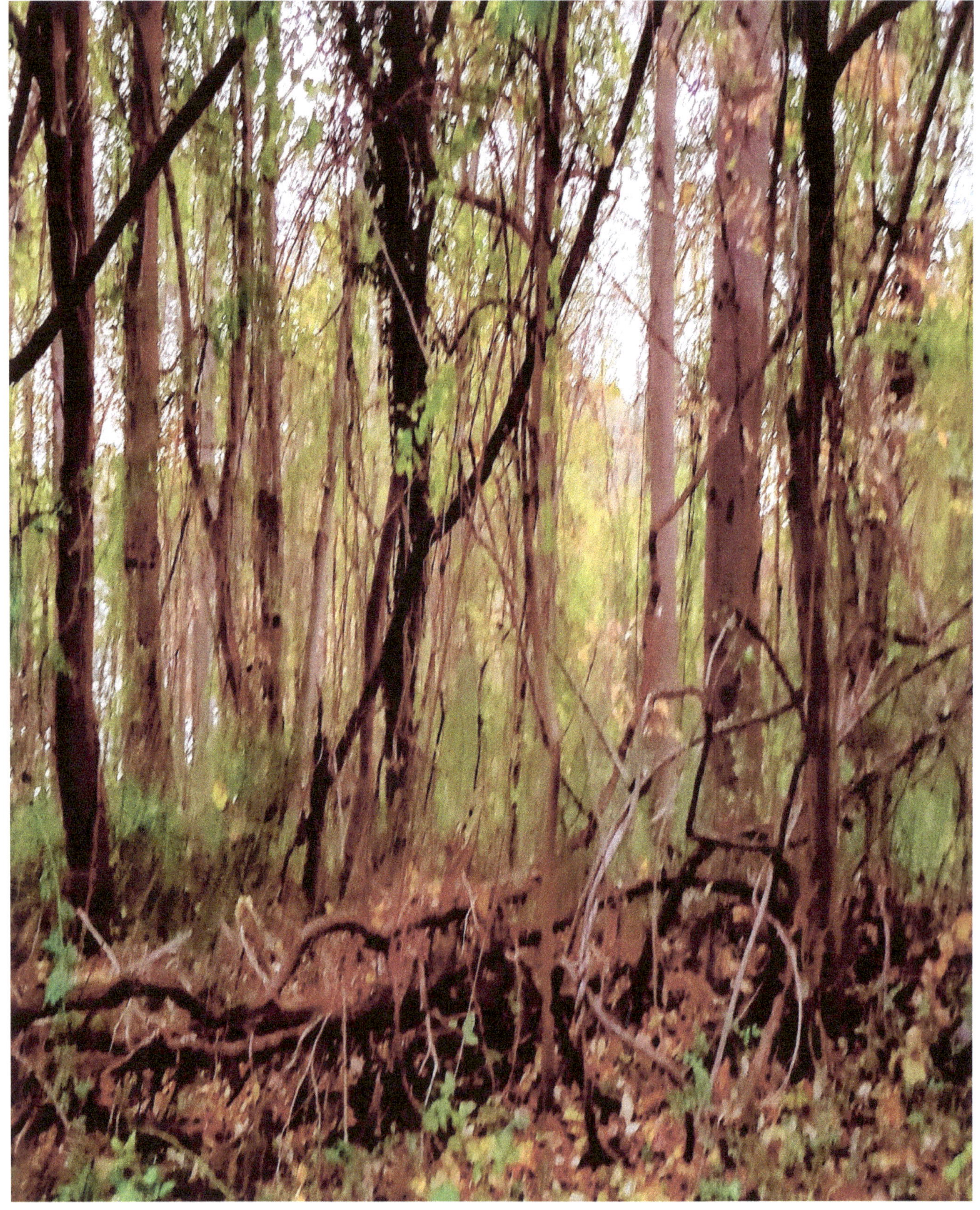

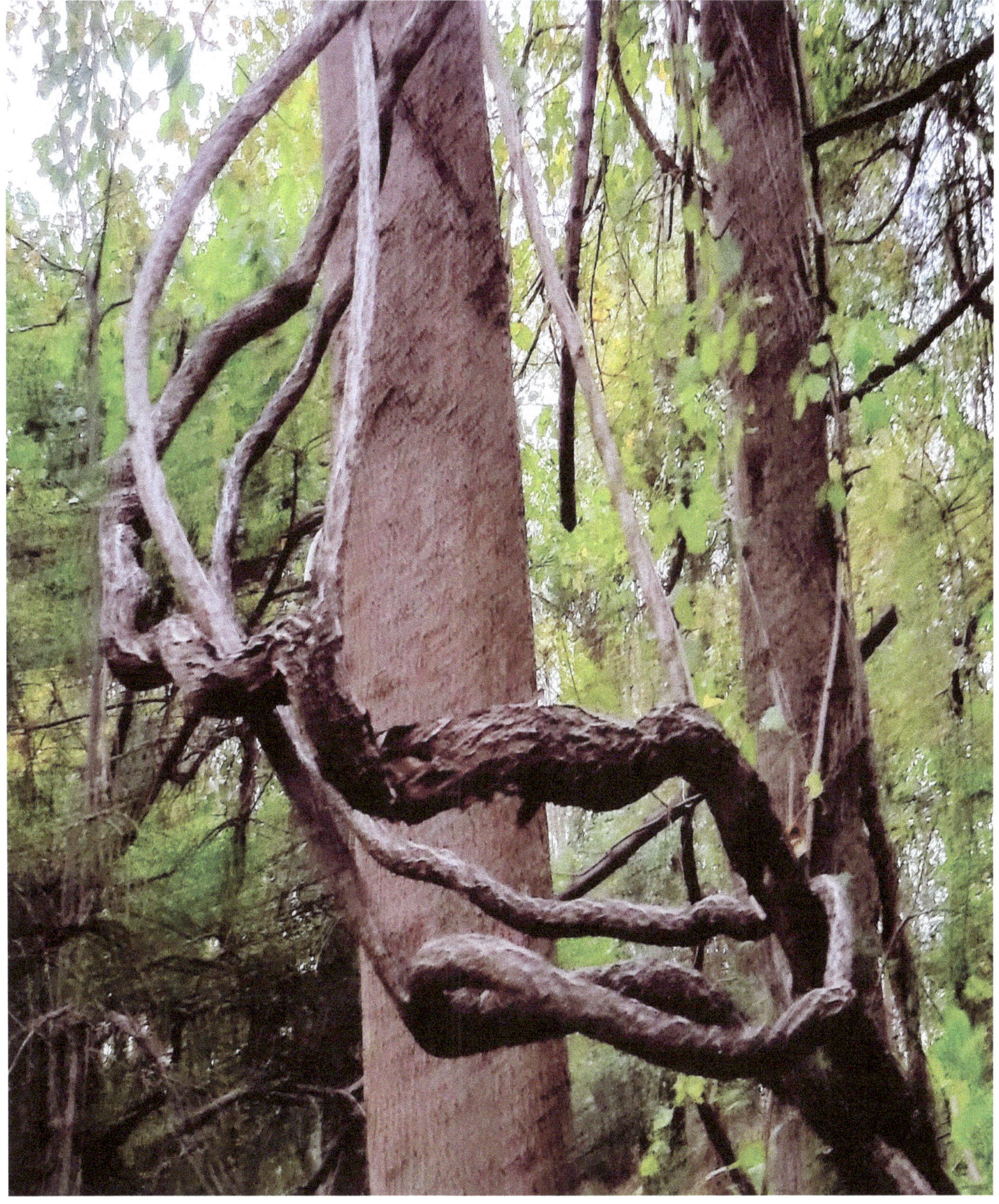

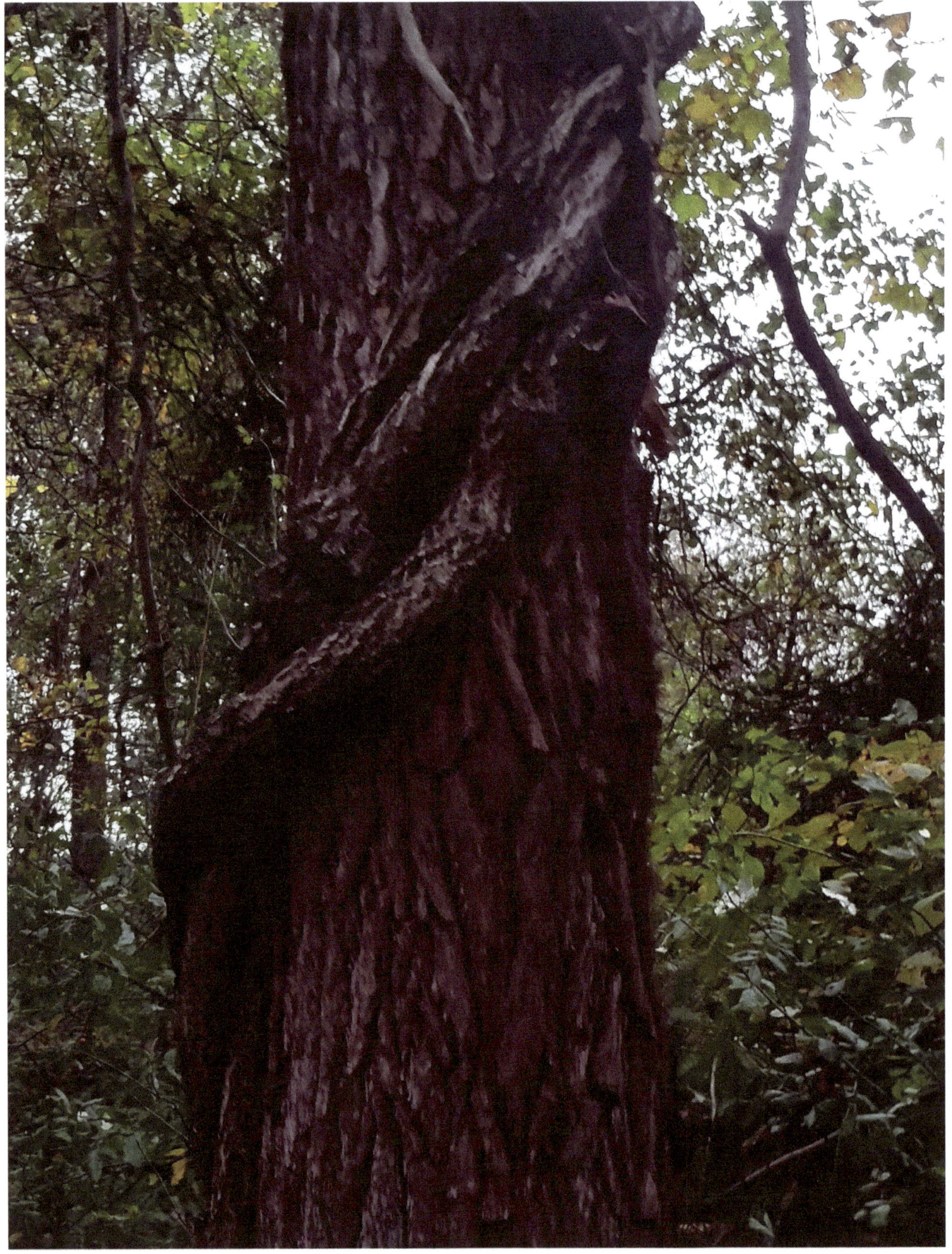

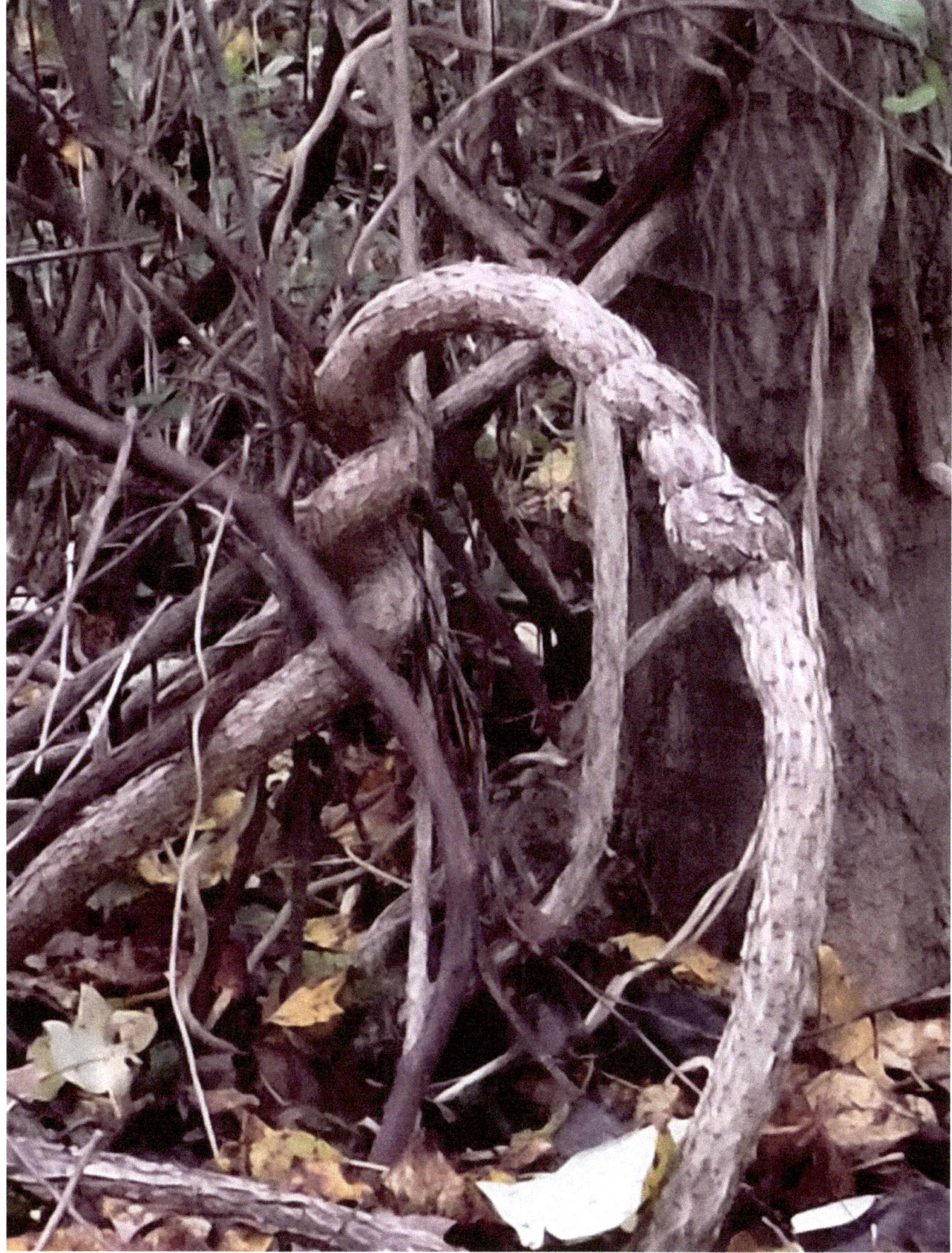

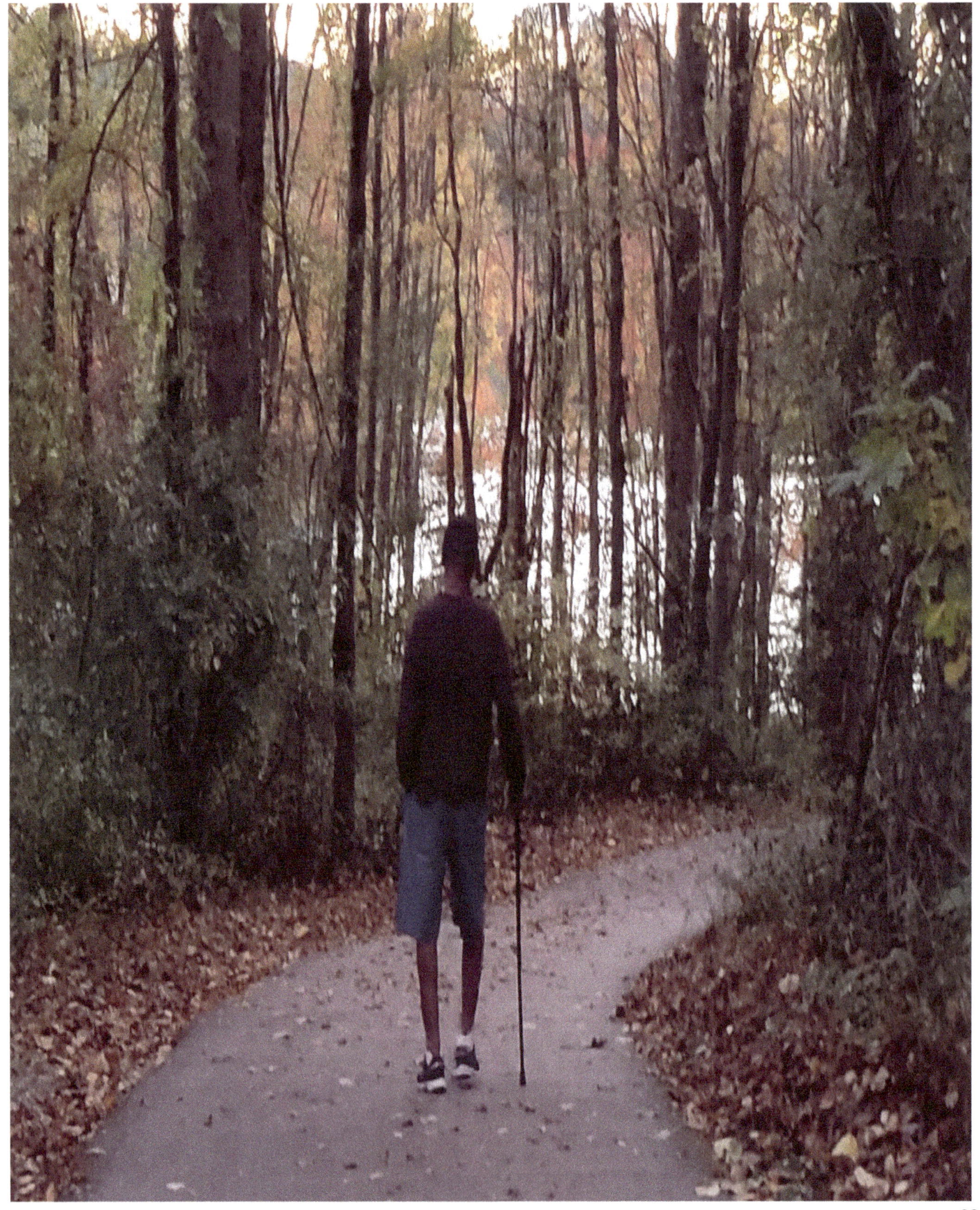

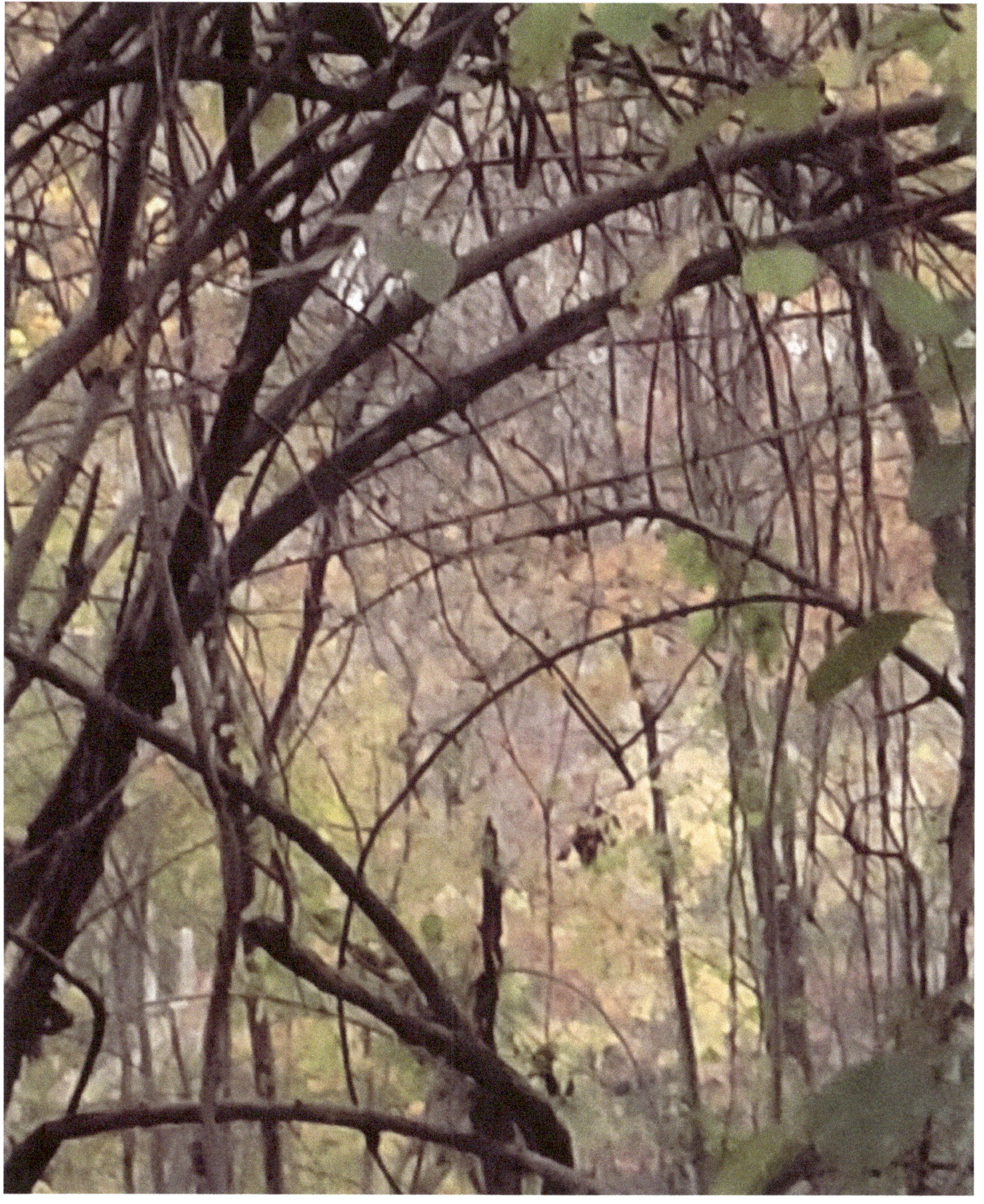

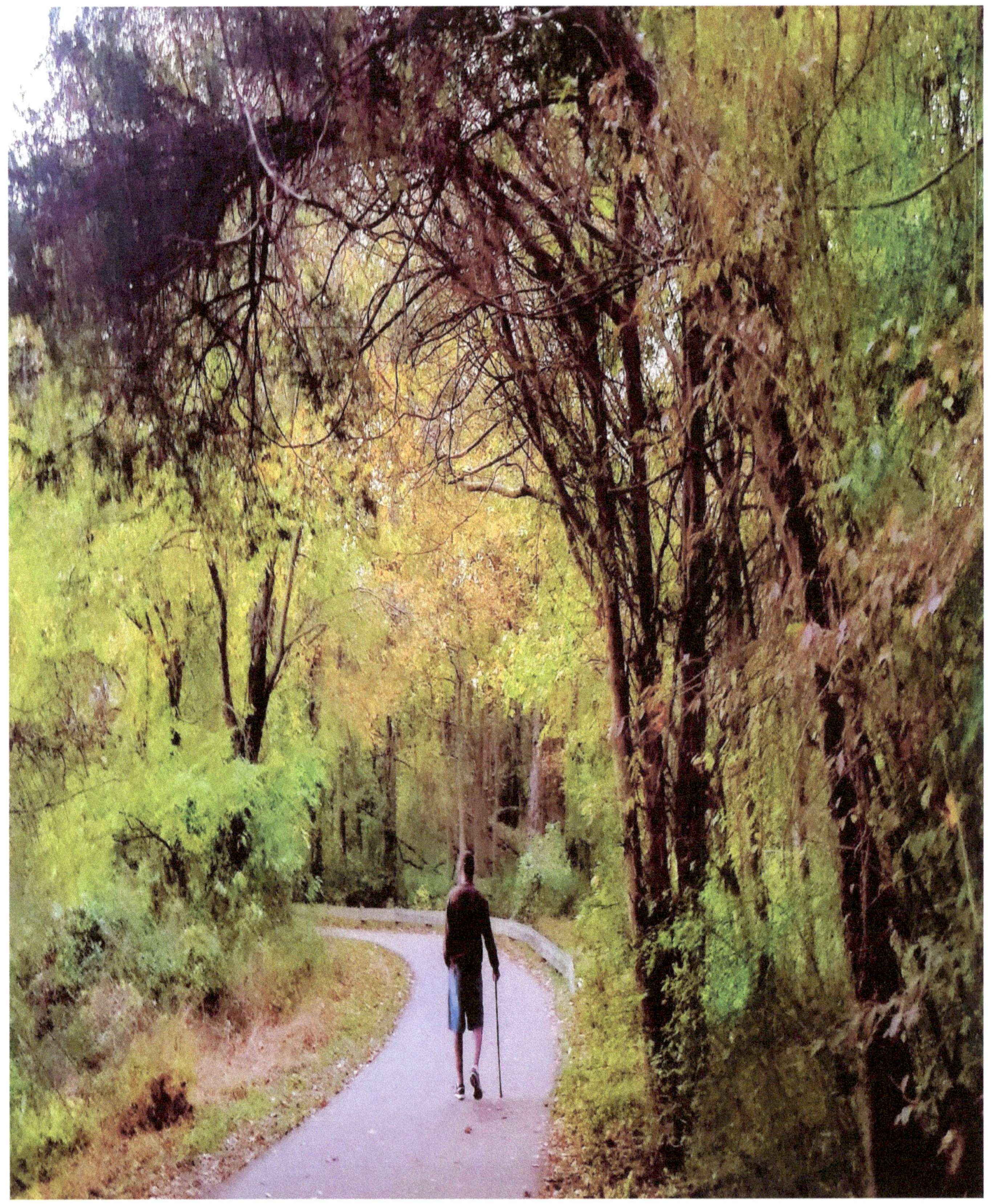

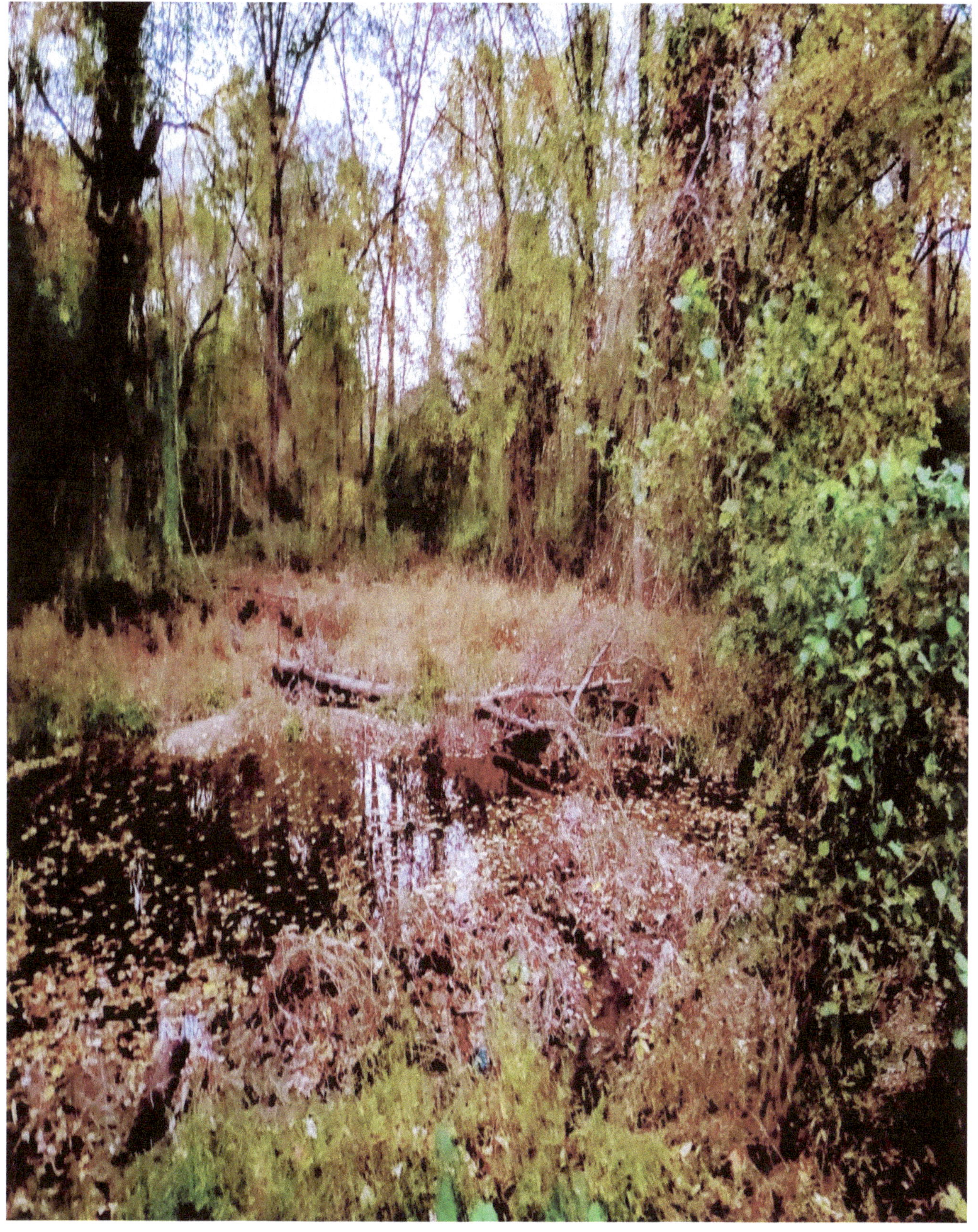

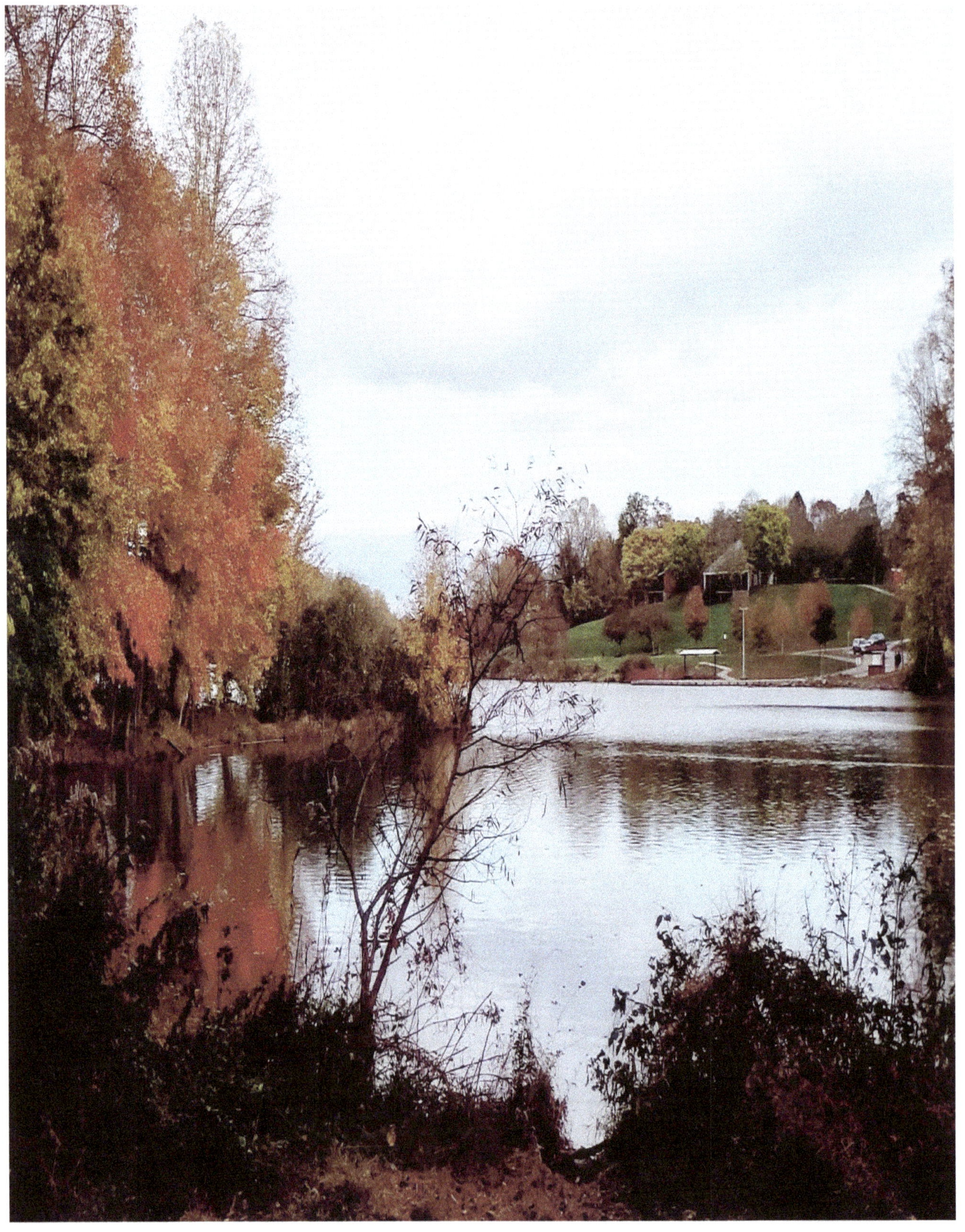

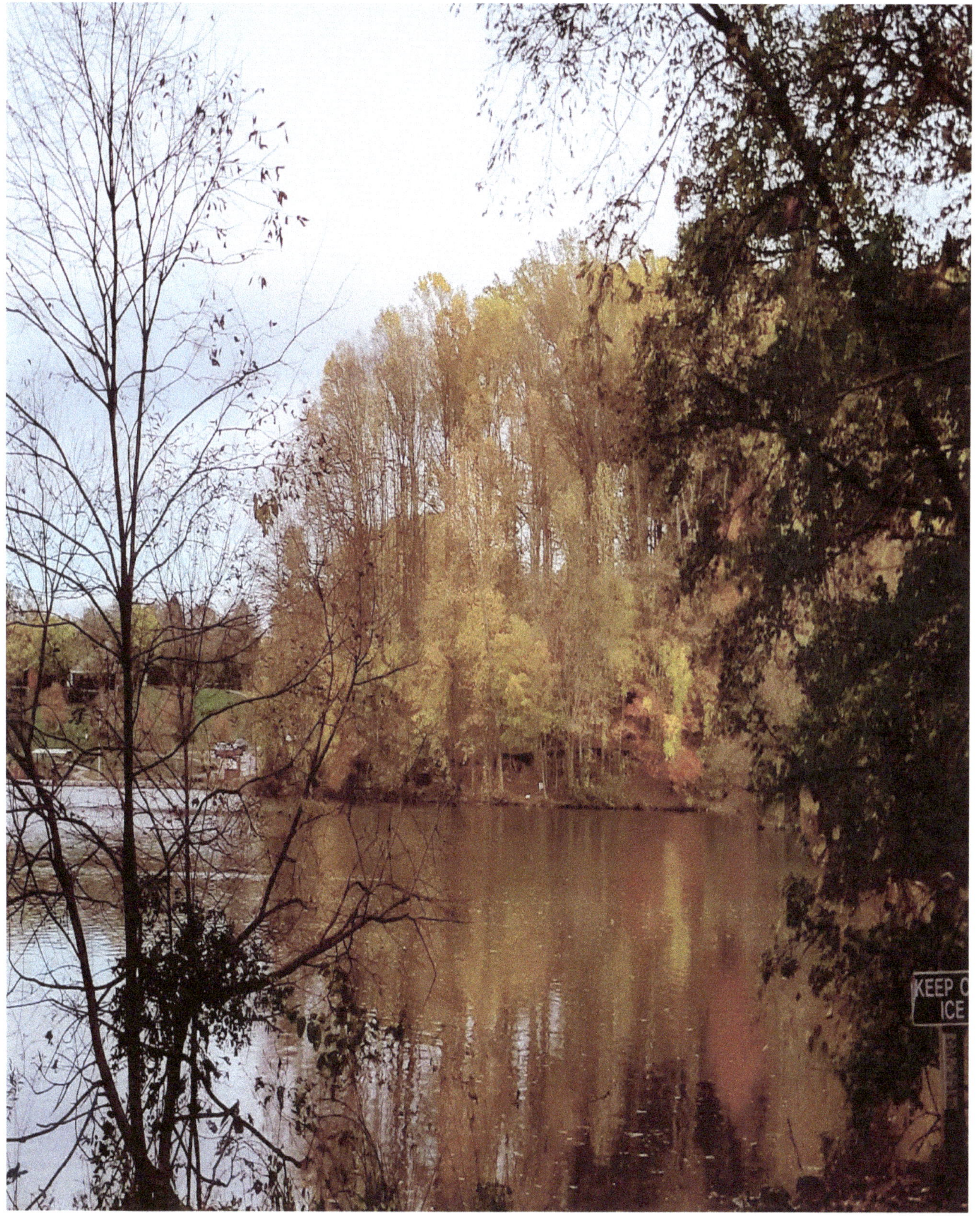

KEEP O
ICE

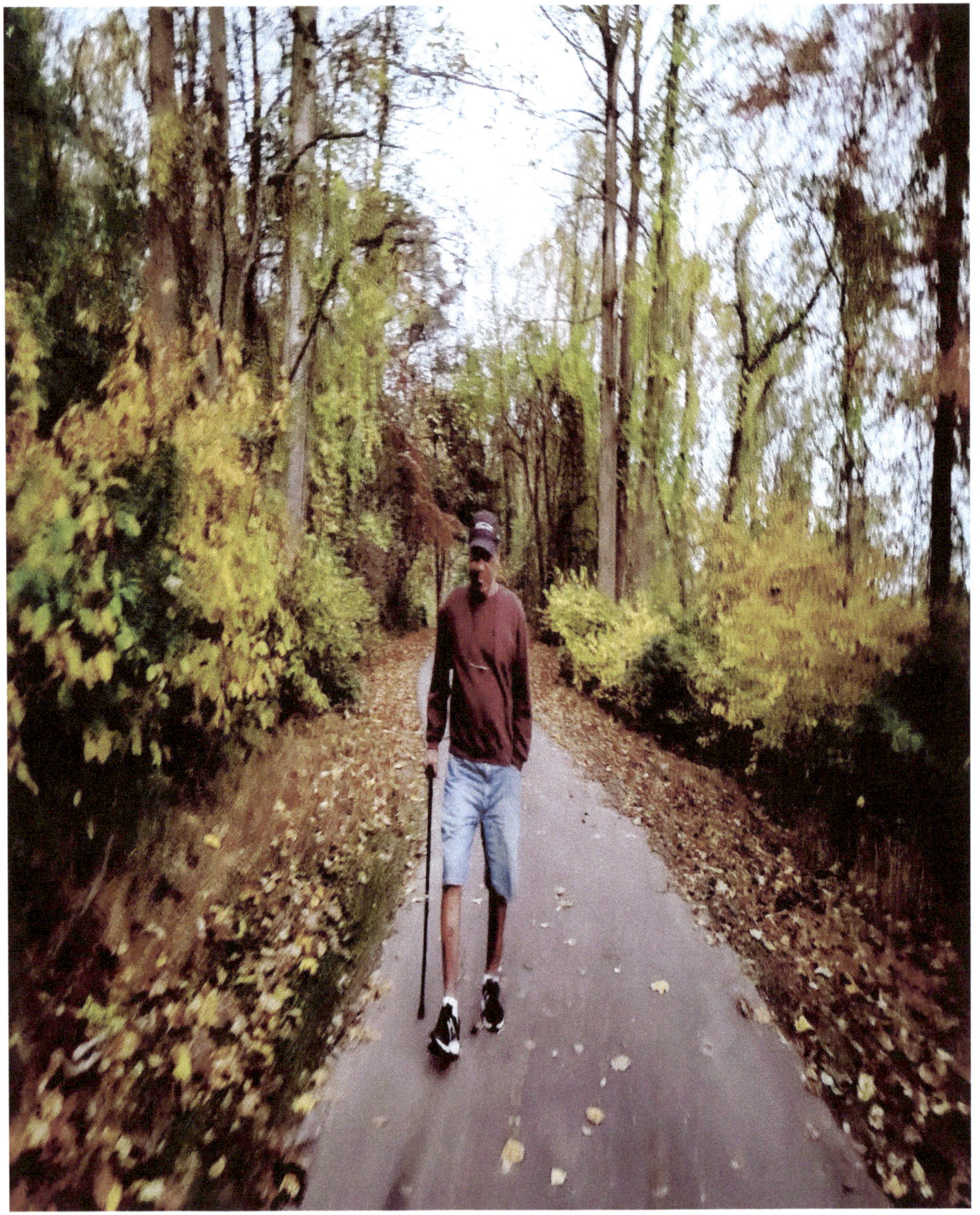

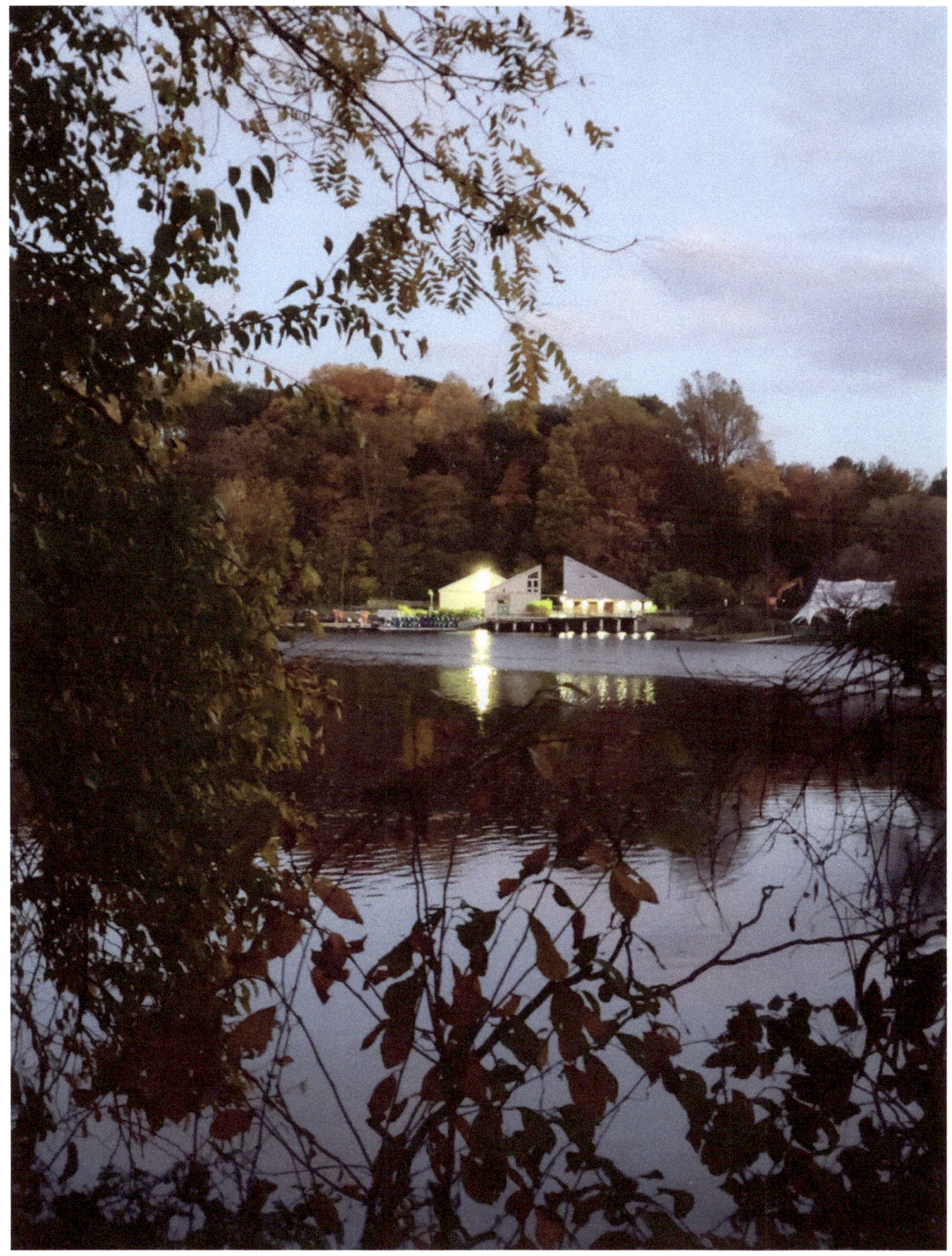

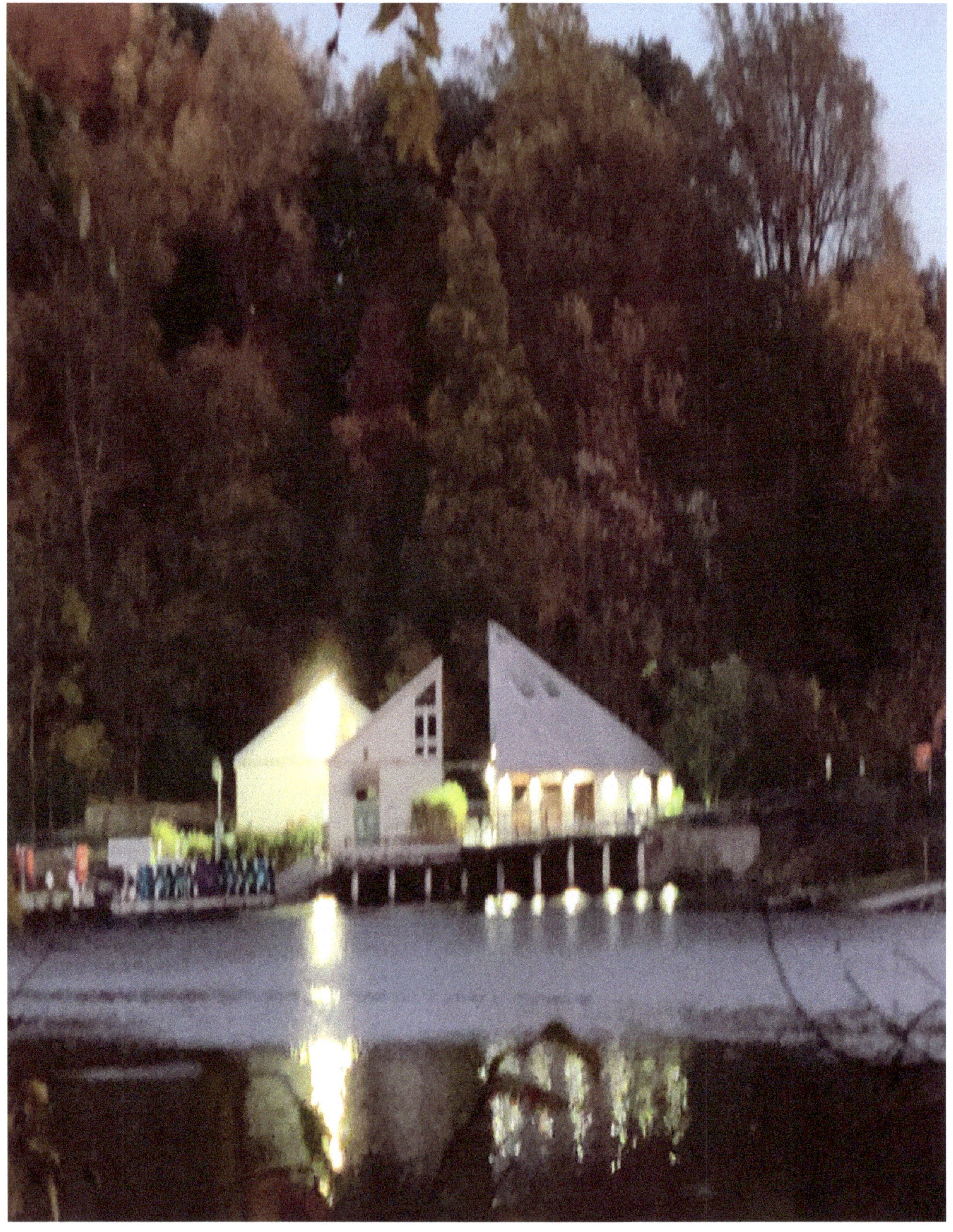

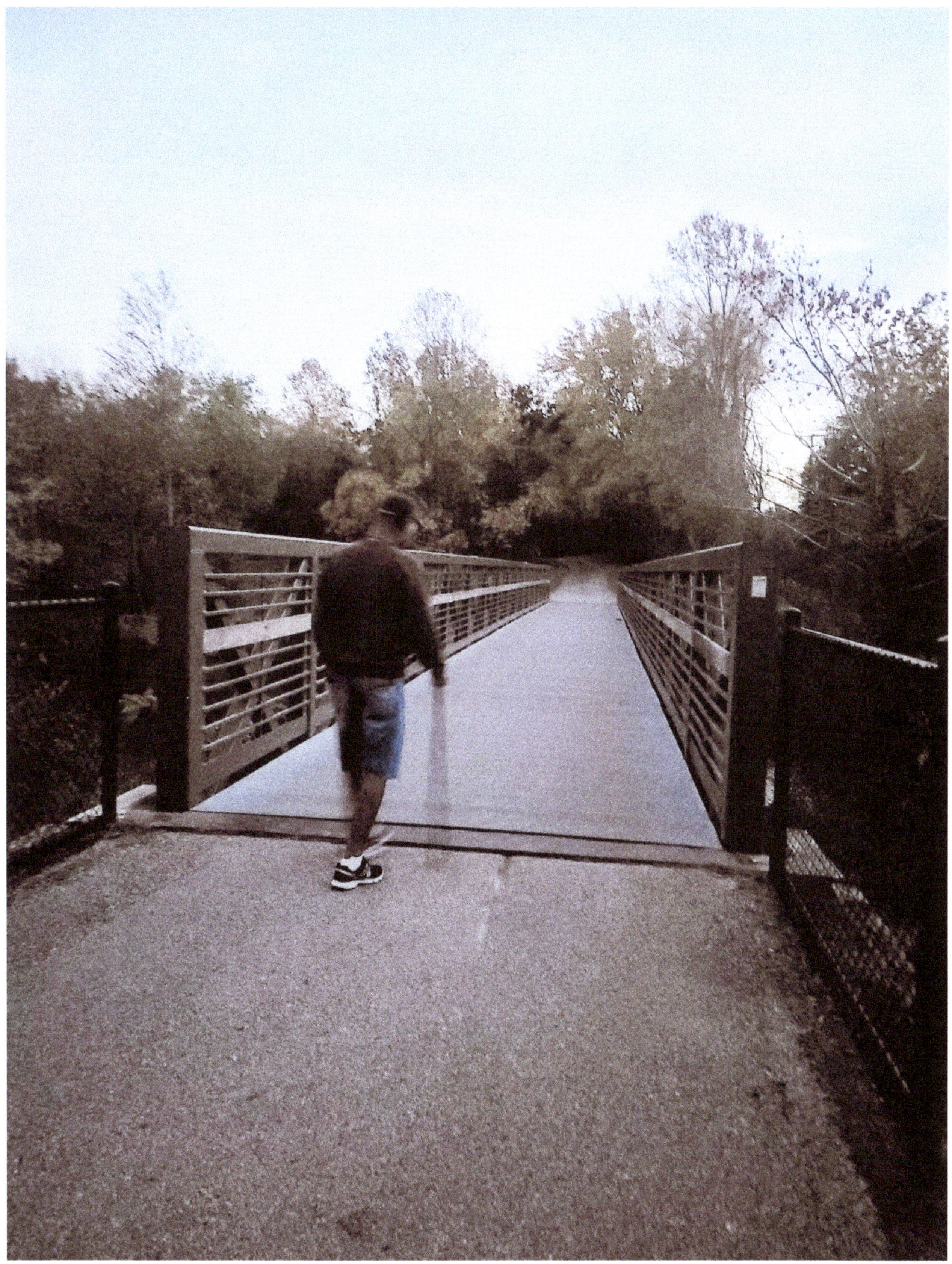

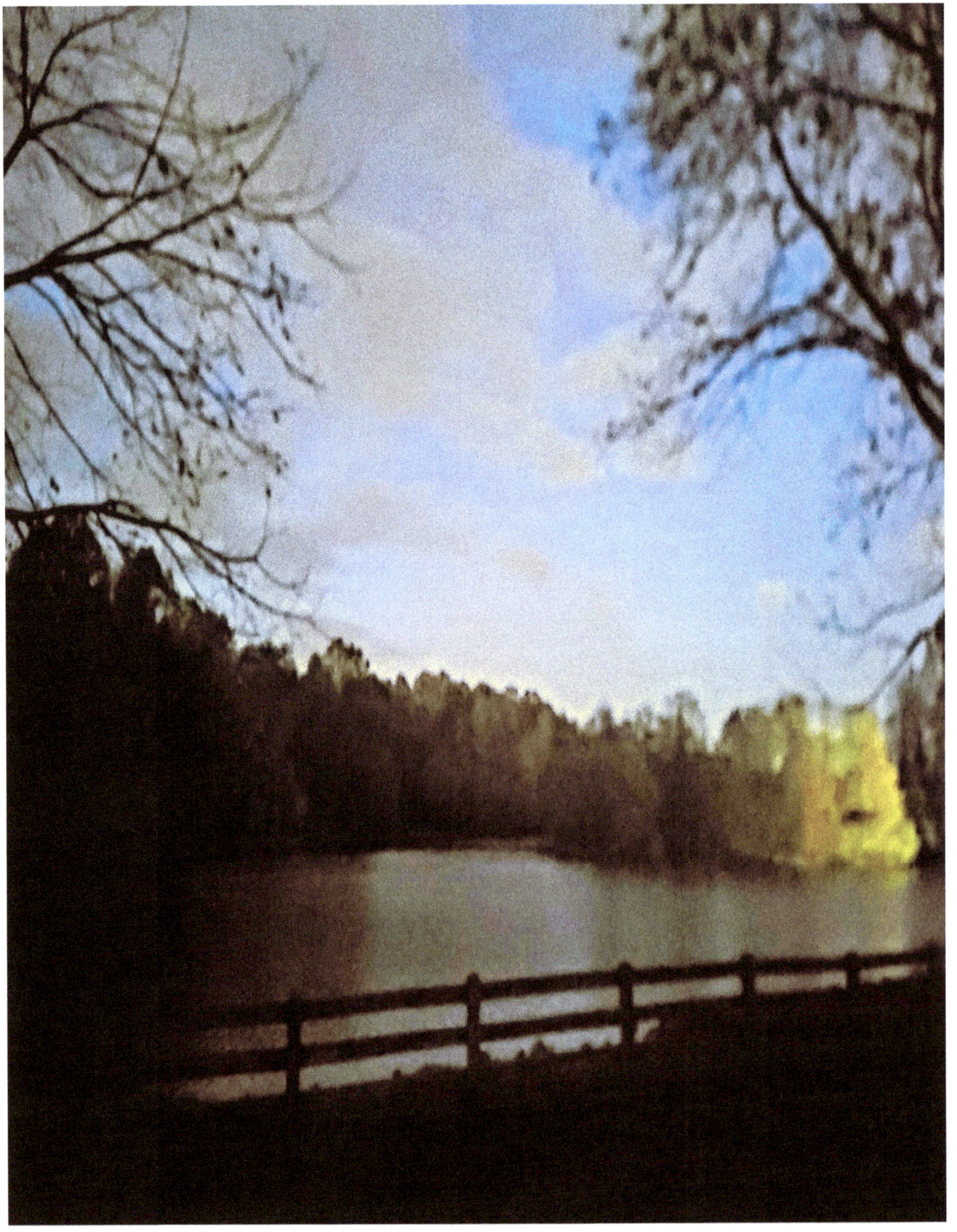

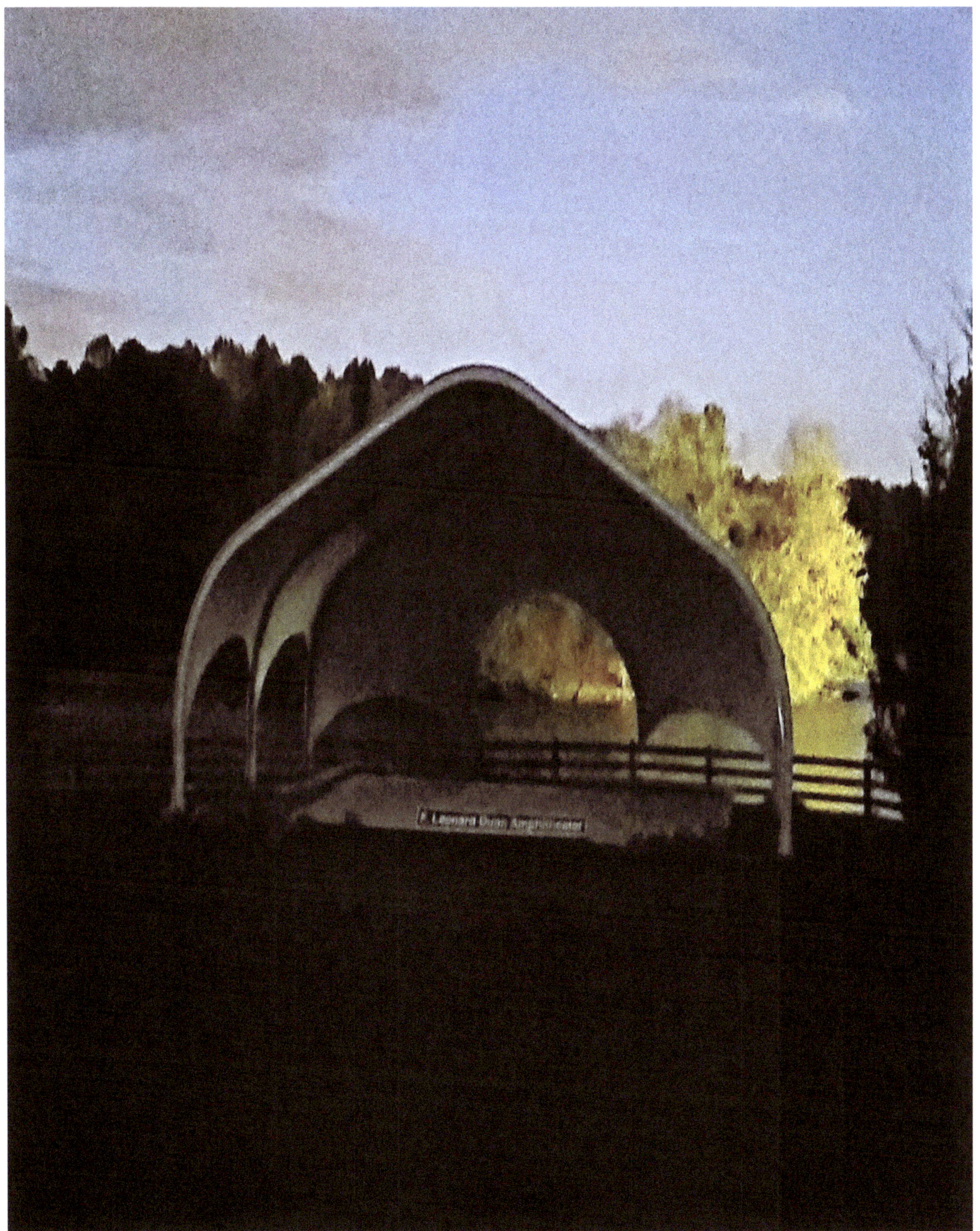
Leonard Dunn Amphitheater

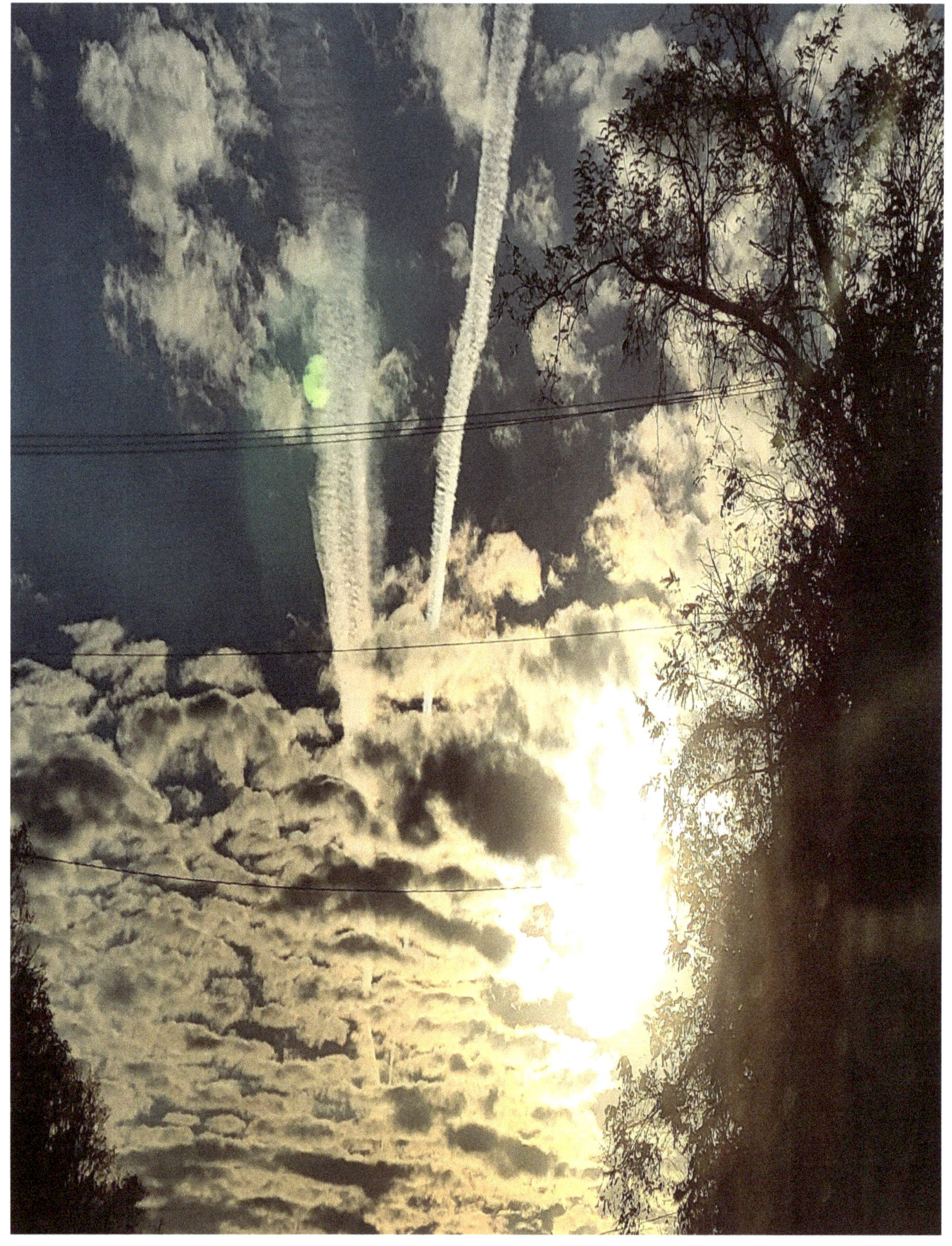

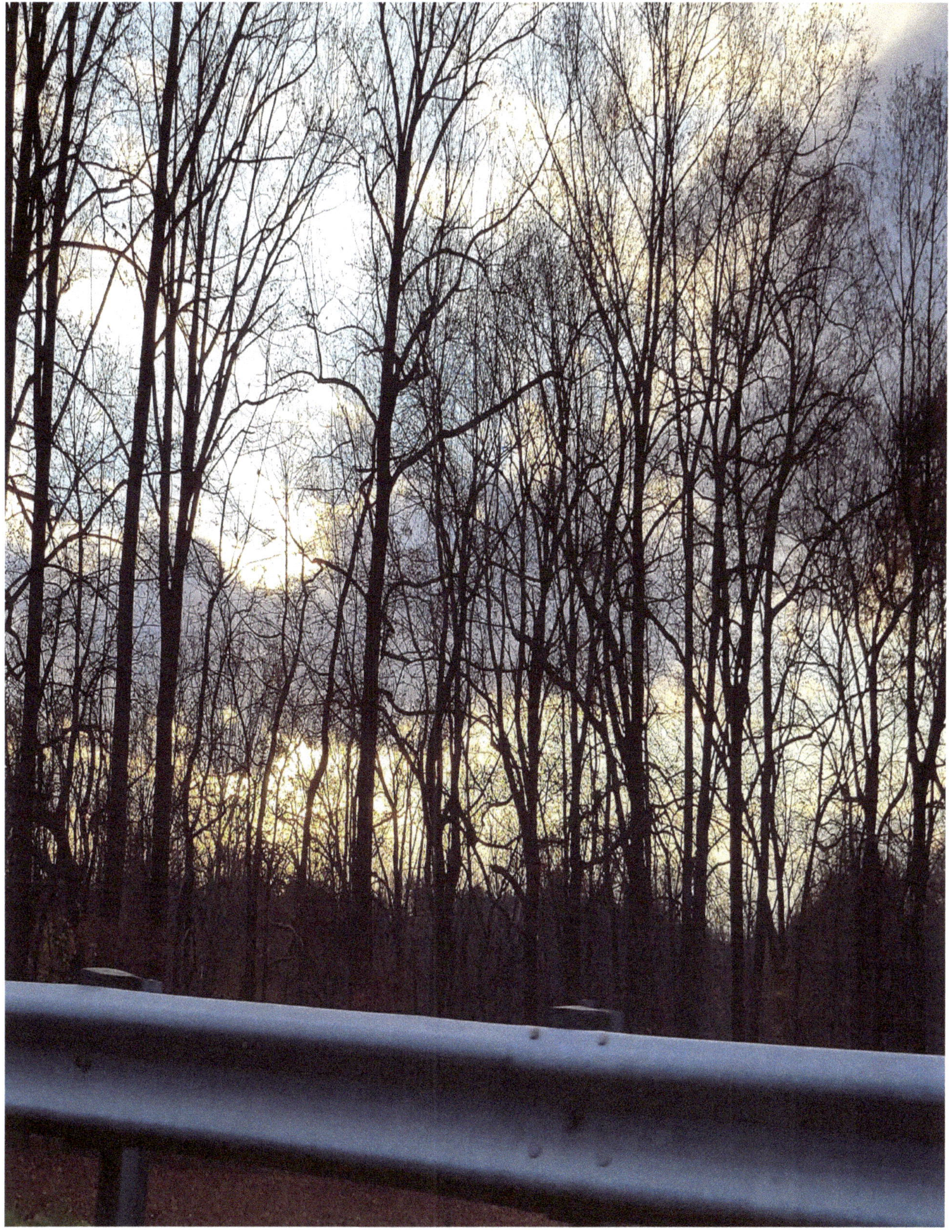

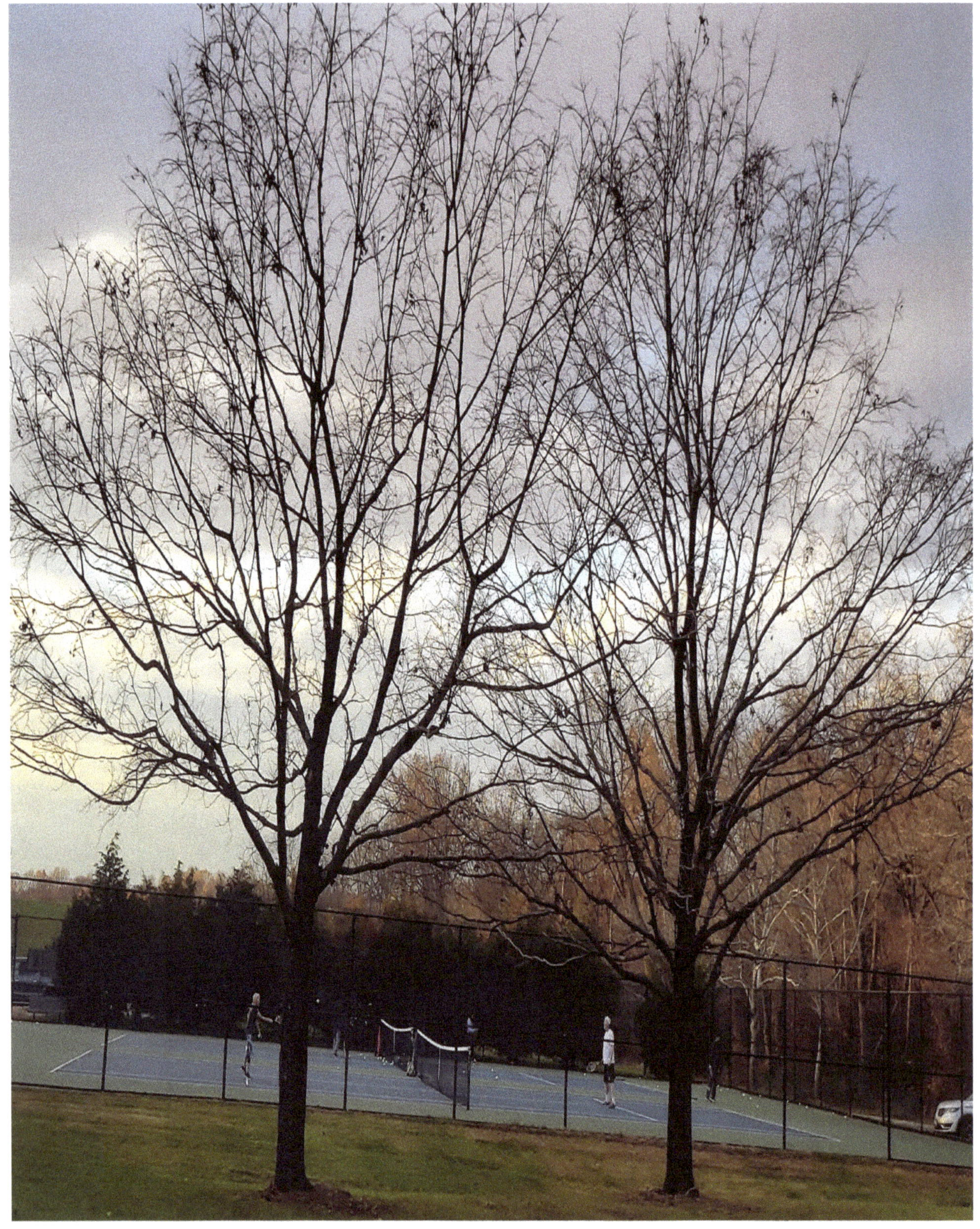

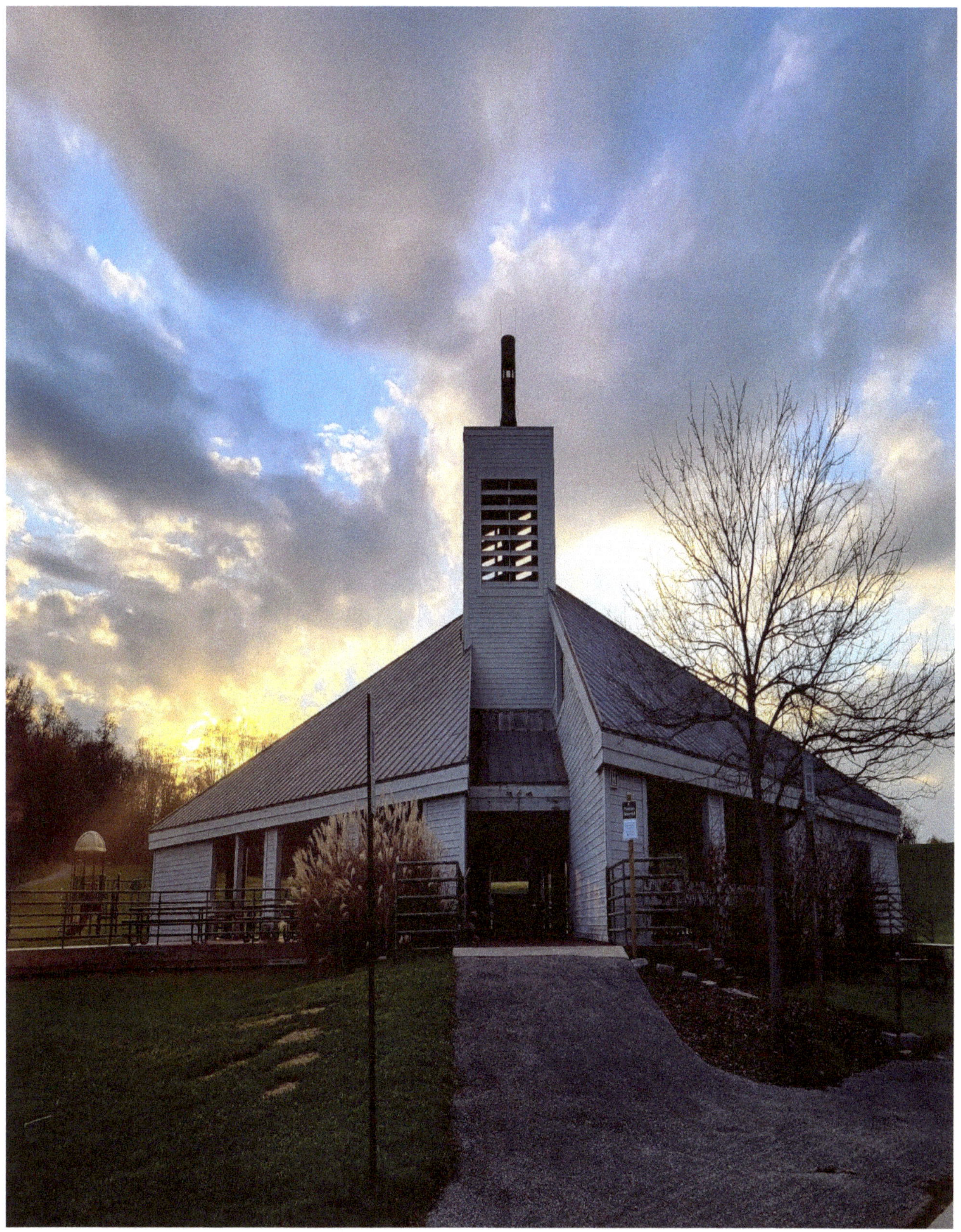

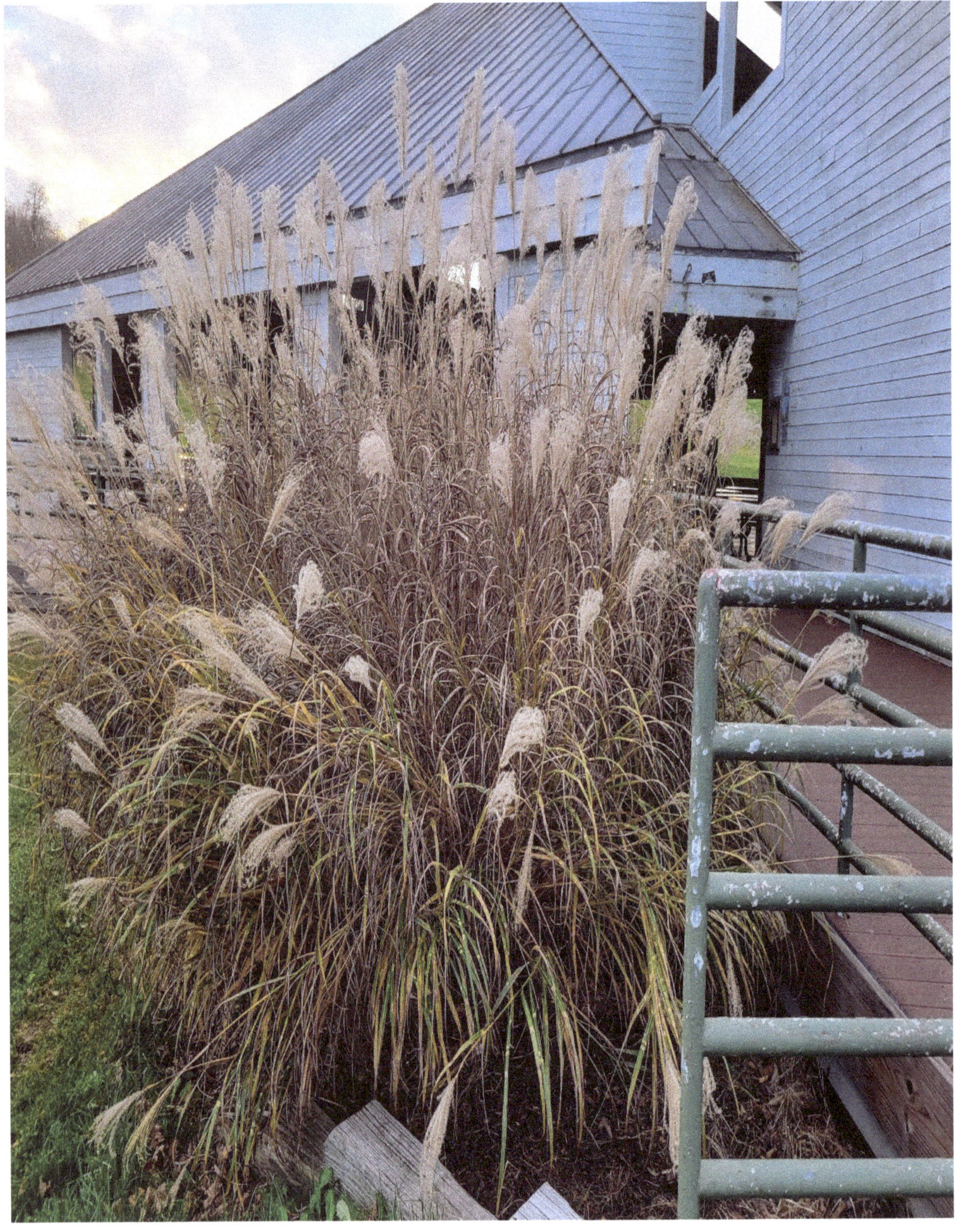

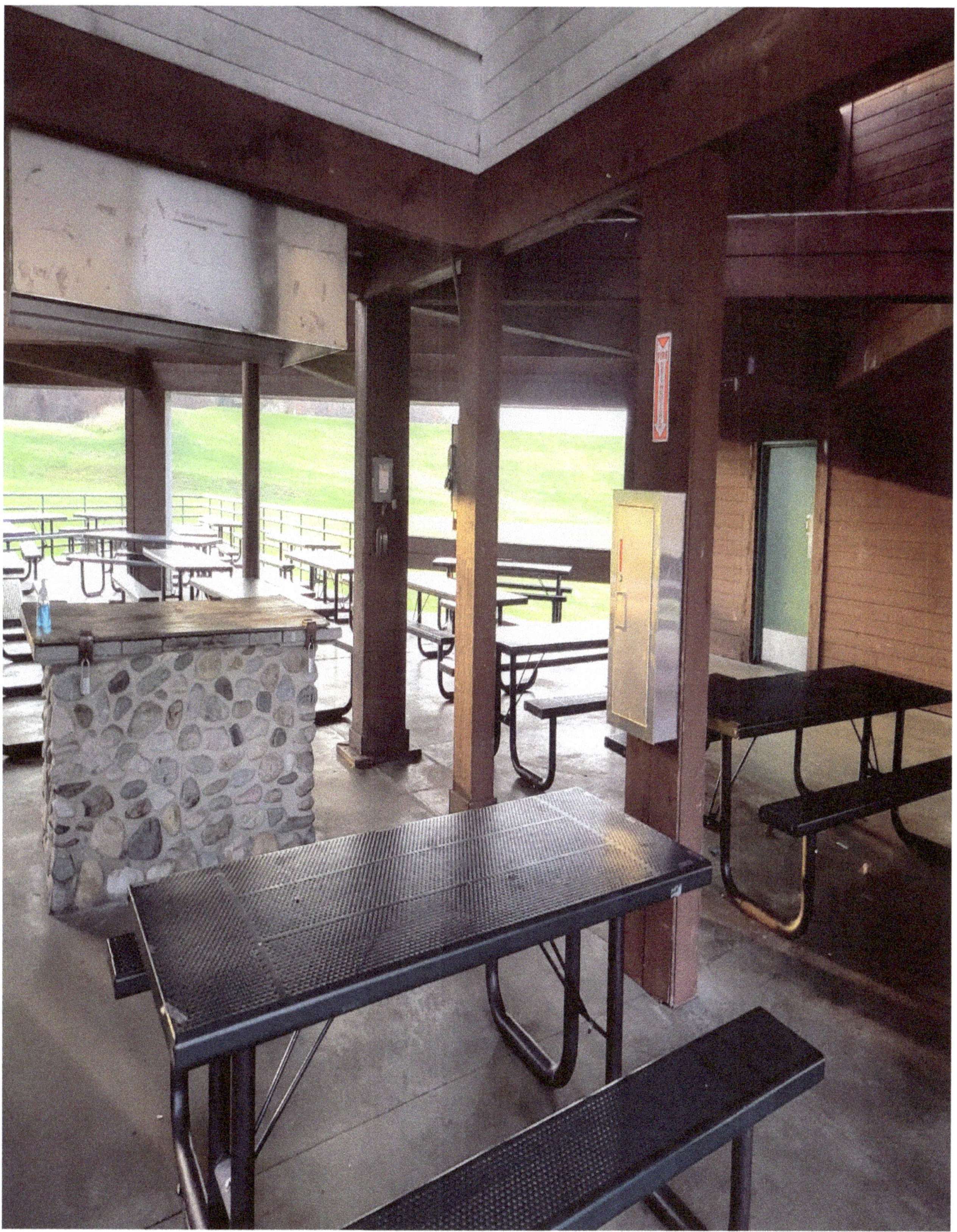

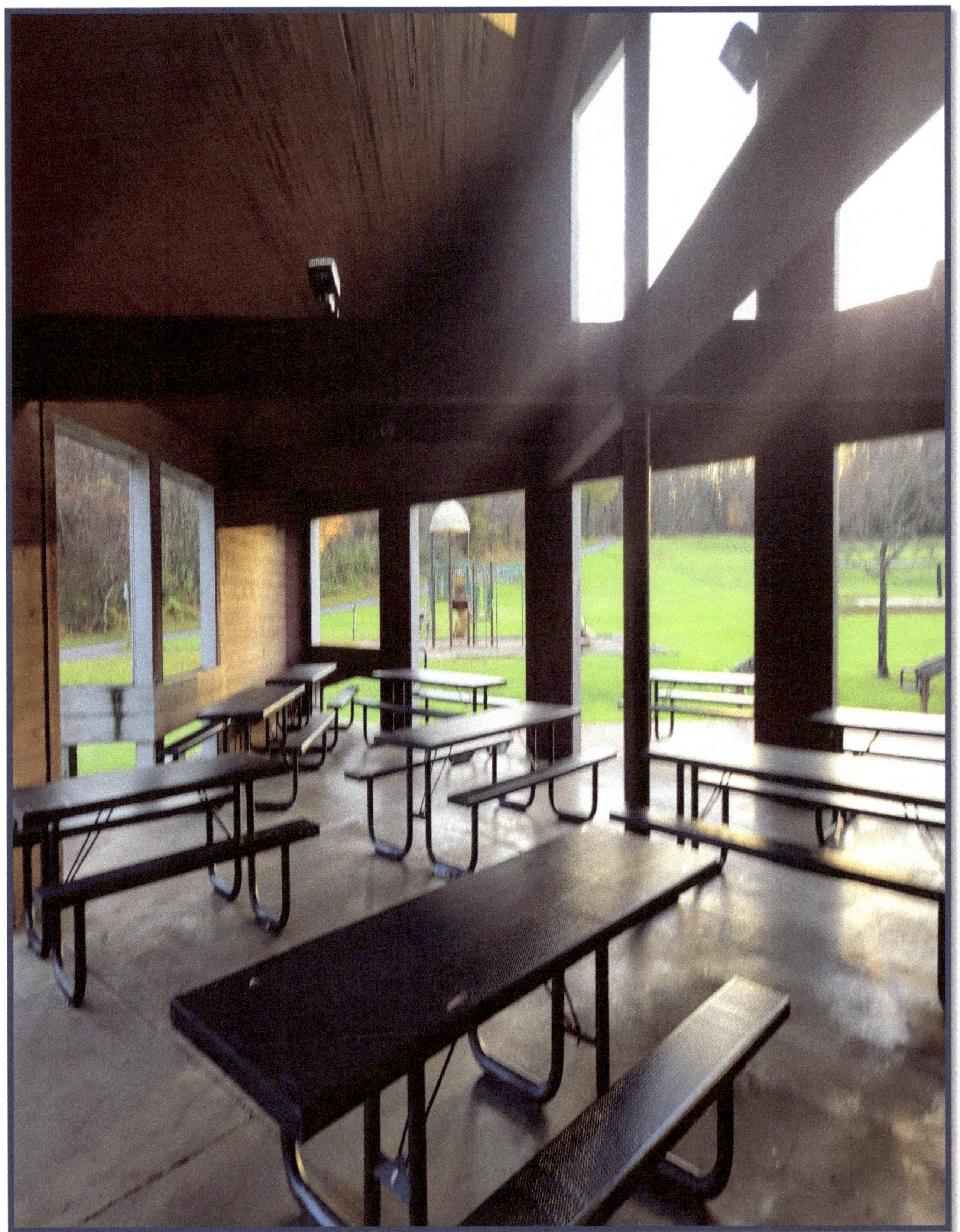

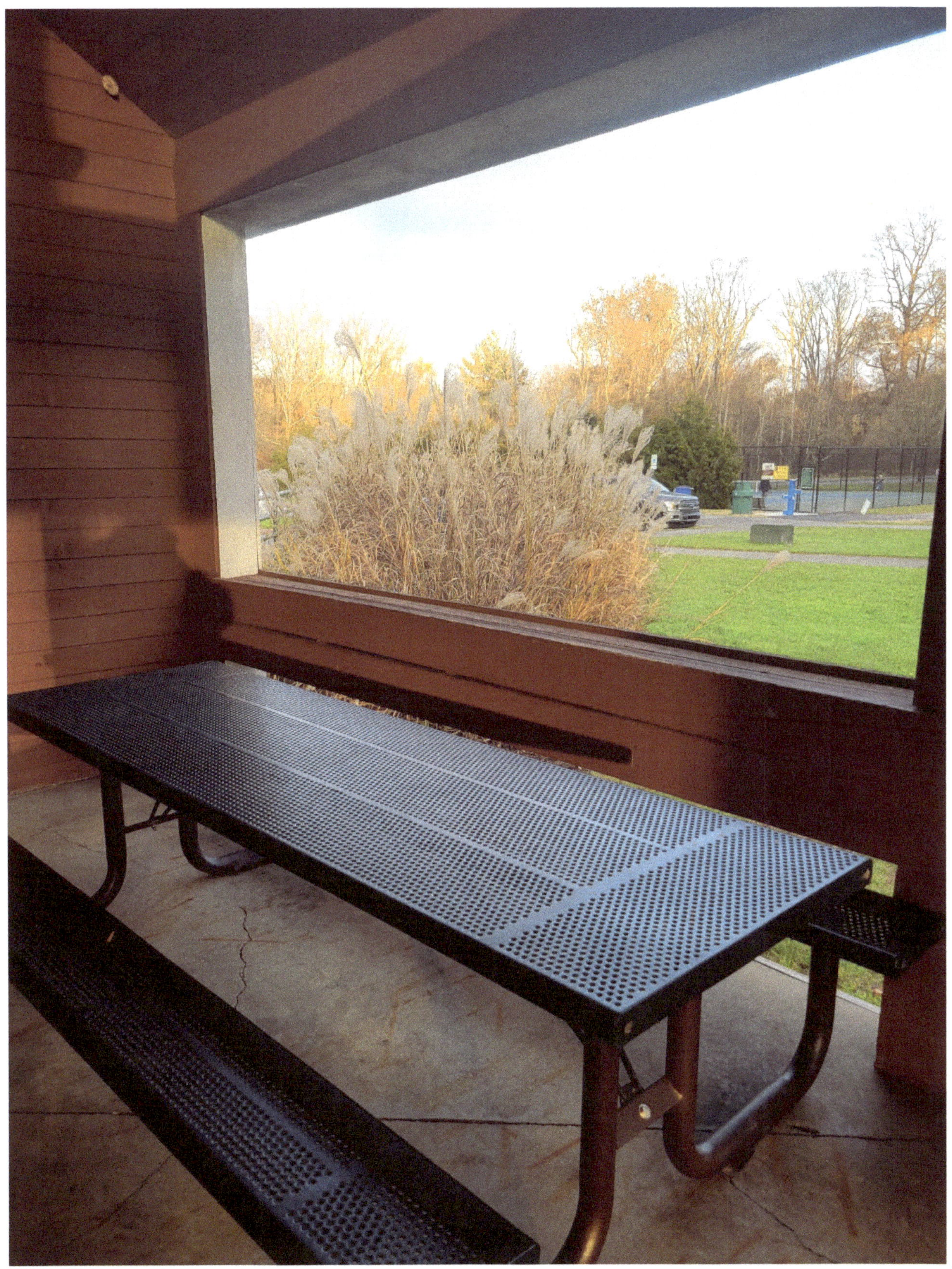

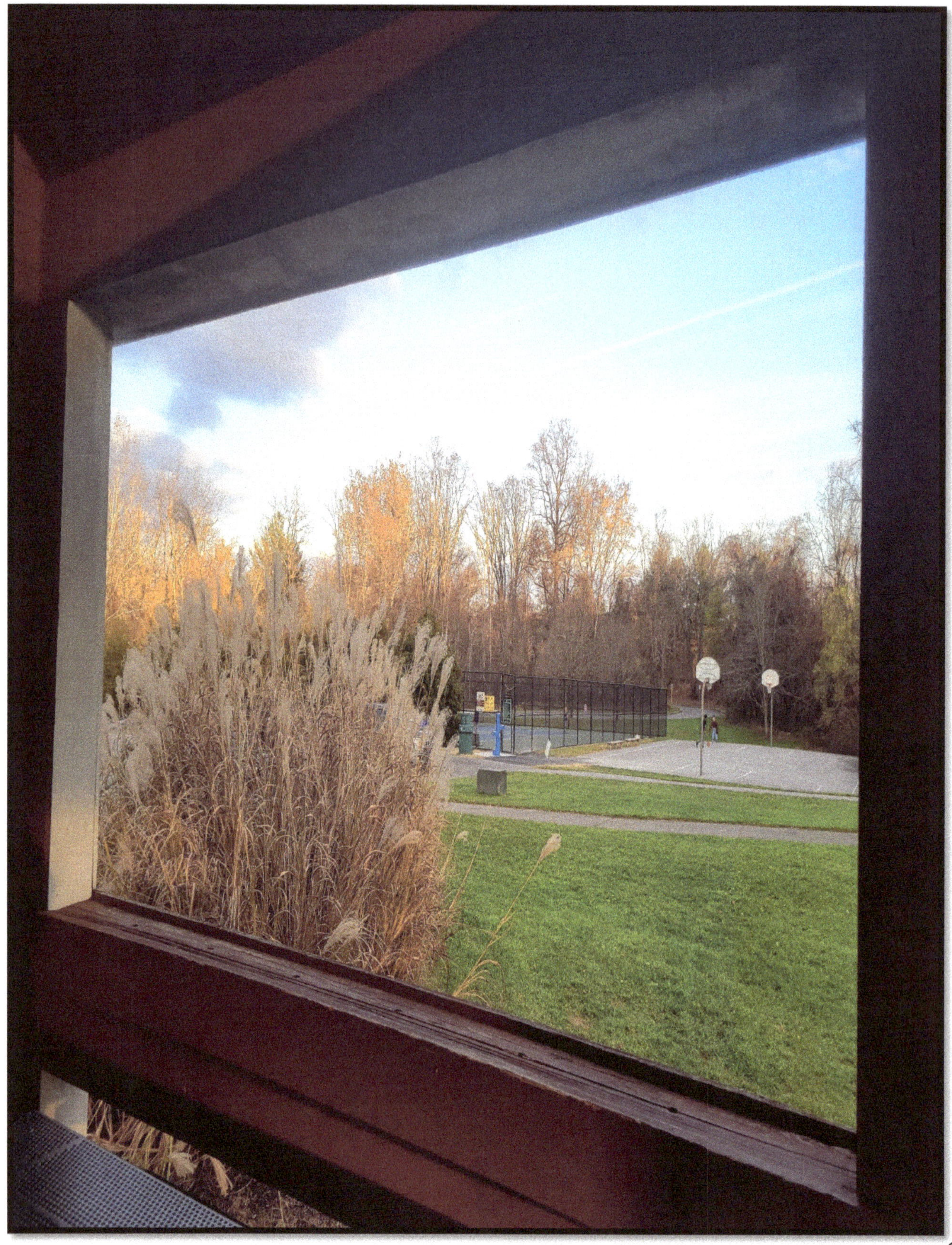

About the Photographer

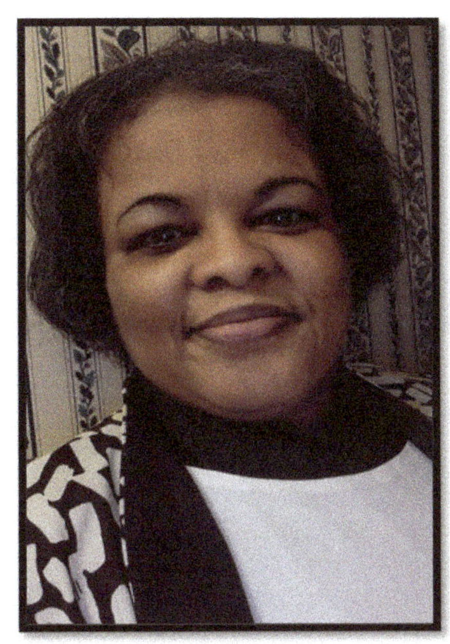

Wynette McKenzie has been an avid photographer since she was a young girl. She studied photography in New York City and in Maryland while pursuing her higher education degree. She has taken countless photographs in her brilliant lifetime.

www.ingramcontent.com/pod-product-compliance
Lightning Source LLC
Chambersburg PA
CBHW041035050726
47599CB00018B/1970